W0067689

DELUGAN MEISSL

ASSOCIATED ARCHITECTS

daab

Introduction   4

Realized Projects

Current Projects

Competitions

The architecture of Delugan Meissl Associated Architects is characterised by an open and sensible approach towards the different building and design tasks of all dimensions. Despite the unquestionable professionalism displayed by the team an experimental outlook is always maintained. Two main architectural strategies determine the work of the Viennese office: the creation of fluent spatial contiguity and the resulting examination of transitional areas and façades.

Space is not primarily regarded as static but rather as a dynamic and variable interaction between people and their environment. A building is always part of an effective spatial relationship. Idiosyncrasies of the location are used as impulses to create an entity which positions itself self-consciously into the context without negating the existing surroundings.

A programmatic delimitation is abolished in favour of a variable organisation of differences, the permeable, intricately distinct or extendable boundary. The strict separation between the interior and exterior becomes subverted, the façade transforms into space and is rendered usable or functions as a filter. Buildings are not considered as mere skins that are to be filled and whose intrinsic flow is blocked through the classical separation into rooms. A sculptural formulation of the exterior produces different spatial valences on the inside which arise out of the formal flux of the architecture.

Space is interpreted along the lines of differing "speeds". Apparent dichotomies such as movement and persistence, intimacy and expanse or security and exposure are brought into a flowing spatial context and linked through differentiated open paths.

Die Architektur von Delugan Meissl Associated Architects kennzeichnet eine offene und sensible Annäherung an die verschiedenen Bauaufgaben unterschiedlicher Dimensionen, die bei aller Professionalität des Teams auch das Interesse am Experimentieren beibehält. Zwei wesentliche architektonische Strategien bestimmen die Arbeit des Wiener Büros: Die Schaffung fließender, offener Raumzusammenhänge und die daraus resultierende Auseinandersetzung mit Übergängen und Fassaden.

Raum wird nicht a priori als statisch, sondern als dynamische und variable Interaktion von Mensch und Umgebung begriffen. Ein Gebäude ist immer Teil eines räumlichen Wirkungszusammenhangs. Das, was dem Ort zu eigen ist, wird als Impuls aufgenommen, um etwas zu erzeugen, das sich selbstbewusst im Kontext positioniert, ohne das Vorhandene zu negieren.

Eine programmatische Abgrenzung wird zugunsten einer variablen Organisation der Unterschiede, der durchlässigen, differenzierten oder erweiterbaren Grenze aufgehoben. Es existiert keine strikte Trennung zwischen innen und außen, flache Fassaden entwickeln sich zu Räumen und werden benutzbar oder fungieren als Filter. Ein Gebäude ist nicht bloße Hülle, die im nach hinein gefüllt und deren innewohnende Bewegung durch klassische Raumaufteilungen behindert wird. Eine plastische Ausformulierung der Außenhaut erzeugt im Gebäudeinneren verschiedene räumliche Wertigkeiten, die sich aus dem Formenverlauf des Baukörpers entwickeln.

Der Raum wird im Sinne unterschiedlicher „Geschwindigkeiten" interpretiert. Scheinbare Gegensätze wie Bewegung und Verharren, Intimität und Weite oder Geborgenheit und Exponiertheit werden in einen fließenden raumgreifenden Zusammenhang gestellt und durch differenziert offene Wegesysteme verknüpft.

Le travail de Delugan Meissl Associated Architects se caractérise par une approche ouverte et sensible des diverses facettes et dimensions de l'architecture, qui témoigne de l'intérêt de cette équipe d'architectes pour une expérimentation qui n'entame en rien leur grand professionnalisme. Deux stratégies architectoniques fondamentales déterminent le travail du studio viennois : la création de rapports spatiaux fluides et la confrontation consécutive avec les transitions et les façades.

L'espace n'est pas compris a priori comme statique, mais en tant qu'interaction dynamique et variable entre l'homme et son environnement. Un édifice est toujours une partie d'un système d'effets spatiaux. Ce qui est propre au lieu est repris comme impulsion, pour produire quelque chose qui se positionne avec assurance dans le contexte, sans nier pour autant ce qui existe déjà.

Les limites qu'impose tout programme s'effacent au profit d'une organisation variable des différences, de la frontière transparente, différenciée ou extensible. Il n'existe pas de séparation stricte entre intérieur et extérieur, les façades plates se muent en espaces et deviennent utilisables, ou tiennent lieu de filtre. Un bâtiment ne se réduit pas à une simple enveloppe que l'on remplirait par la suite et dont le mouvement inhérent serait handicapé par une distribution conventionnelle des pièces. La formulation plastique de la peau extérieure produit à l'intérieur de la construction diverses valeurs spatiales qui découlent de l'évolution formelle du corps de bâtiment.

L'espace est interprété au sens de différentes « vitesses ». Les oppositions apparentes telles que mouvement et statisme, volumes intimes et volumes larges, ou encore refuge et étalage sont placées dans un rapport spatial fluide et unies par des voies de déambulation dont l'ouverture est nuancée.

Una aproximación abierta y sensible a las diferentes tareas constructivas de diversas dimensiones caracteriza la arquitectura de Delugan Meissl Associated Architects, la cual con toda la profesionalidad del equipo mantiene también el interés por la experimentación. Dos estrategias arquitectónicas fundamentales determinan el trabajo del despacho de Viena: la creación de relaciones espaciales abiertas y fluidas, y el consecuente análisis de tránsitos y fachadas.

El espacio no se concibe a priori como algo estático, sino como una interacción variable y dinámica de ser humano y entorno. Un edificio forma parte siempre de un estímulo espacial. Lo que es intrínseco a un lugar se capta como impulso para realizar algo, que ocupe conscientemente su posición en el contexto sin negar lo ya existente.

Se prescinde de una limitación programática en favor de una organización variable de las diferencias, de la frontera permeable, diferenciada o ampliable. No existe separación estricta entre interior y exterior, fachadas planas se transforman en espacios y se vuelven utilizables, o actúan como filtro. Un edificio no es mera envoltura que se percibe posteriormente y cuyo movimiento íntimo se obstaculiza con las clásicas distribuciones espaciales. La conformación de la piel exterior engendra en el interior del edificio diferentes valencias espaciales que evolucionan a partir del desarrollo formal del cuerpo constructivo.

El edificio se interpreta en el sentido de "velocidades" distintas. Conceptos aparentemente opuestos como movimiento y permanencia, intimidad y extensión, recogimiento y exteriorización entablan una conexión amplia y fluida, y se enlazan mediante itinerarios diferenciados y abiertos.

L'architettura di Delugan Meissl Associated Architects si contraddistingue per l'approccio aperto e sensibile ai vari incarichi di costruzione di dimensioni diverse e coniuga l'interesse per la sperimentazione con la professionalità del gruppo dei collaboratori. Due fondamentali strategie architettoniche determinano il lavoro dello studio viennese: la creazione di contesti spaziali aperti e fluidi e il conseguente confronto con passaggi e facciate.

Lo spazio non è a priori statico, ma un'interazione dinamica e variabile tra uomo e ambiente. Un edificio fa sempre parte di una relazione spaziale di effetti. Ciò che è proprio del luogo serve come impulso per creare qualcosa di nuovo, che si colloca fieramente nel contesto, senza negare ciò che già era presente.

Si rinuncia ad una delimitazione programmatica a favore di un'organizzazione variabile delle differenze, dei confini permeabili, differenziati o ampliabili. Non esiste nessuna divisione netta tra interno ed esterno, facciate piane diventano ambienti utilizzabili o fungono da filtro. Un edificio non è un semplice guscio, che si riempie in un secondo momento e il cui moto insito è ostacolato dalla classica distribuzione dei vani. Un completamento in senso plastico del rivestimento esterno crea all'interno del palazzo diverse valenze di spazi derivanti dall'andamento delle forme del fabbricato.

Lo spazio viene interpretato secondo "velocità" diverse. Opposti apparenti come movimento e attesa, intimità e vastità o sicurezza ed esposizione vengono posti in un'ampia relazione fluida e collegati per mezzo di sistemi di percorso differenziati ed aperti.

REALIZED PROJECTS

CURRENT PROJECTS

COMPETITIONS

HOUSE RAY 1
SINGLE FAMILY HOUSE / ROOFTOP EXPANSION | VIENNA
Address: Mittersteig 10, 1050 Vienna
Client: Delugan Meissl
Construction period: 2001-2003
Floor area: 230 m^2
Photocredits: R. Steiner, H. Hurnaus, P. Rigaud

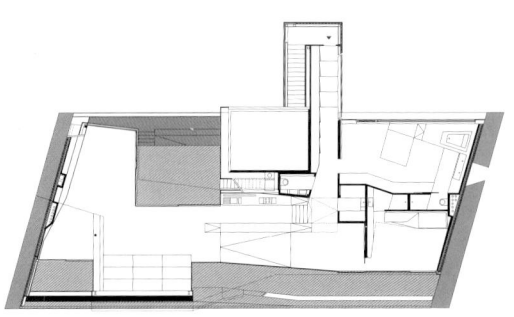

Situated on the flat roof of a 1960s office building amidst the rooftop landscape of Vienna's fourth district, Ray 1 evolved out of the direct effectual relationship and spatial quality of the location. This origin, however, is by no means contradicted by the clash of the static mass and the dynamic form of architecture in motion; on the contrary, this juxtaposition serves to charge the structure. The new building is generated out of the connection between the two adjoining buildings, continuing the line of projection of the gables and providing the missing link. The boundary between sky and earth, however, is not understood to be a dividing line separating the roof and the surrounding context, but as a permeable border zone that becomes living space itself. Incisions and superimpositions create transparent zones and sheltered terraced landscapes on both sides of the building that enable the experience of the exposed situation, from the entrance all the way up to the accessible roof area. The outer skin, which is coated with Alucobond, defines the contours of the apartment's interior, suggesting varying valences for different zones and niches. The intention was to create a shell that would function as a programmable medium for furniture or rather to transform the furniture through the architecture. The interior space is designed as a spacious loft whose various functional areas are defined by folds and different floor levels.

Ray 1, in der Dachlandschaft des vierten Wiener Bezirks auf dem Flachdach eines Bürogebäudes aus den 60er Jahren gelegen, generiert sich zunächst aus diesem unmittelbaren Wirkungszusammenhang und der räumlichen Qualität des Ortes. Dabei wird in der Begegnung von statischem Körper und dynamischer Form bewegter Architektur, der Ursprung keineswegs verleugnet, sondern in eben diesem Aufeinandertreffen aufgeladen. Der Neubau entwickelt sich aus der Verbindung der beiden angrenzenden Gebäude, indem er die Giebellinie fortführt und gewissermaßen den *missing link* herstellt. Die Demarkationslinie zwischen Himmel und Erde wird hier jedoch nicht als abschließende Trennung von Dach und umgebendem Kontext verstanden, sondern als durchlässige Grenze, die dabei selbst zum Lebensraum wird. Einschnitte und Überlagerungen bilden transparente Bereiche und geschützte Terrassenlandschaften zu beiden Seiten des Gebäudes aus, die die exponierte Lage bis hin zum begehbaren Dach erlebbar machen. Die mit Alucobond beschichtete Außenhaut formuliert im Innenraum plastisch unterschiedliche Wertigkeiten verschiedener Zonen und Nischen. Dabei war es das Ziel, die Gebäudehülle zu einem Datenträger für Möbel auszubilden beziehungsweise diese aus der Architektur heraus zu transformieren: Der Innenraum gestaltet sich als großzügiges Loft, dessen unterschiedliche Funktionsbereiche durch Auffaltungen und Höhendifferenzierungen definiert werden.

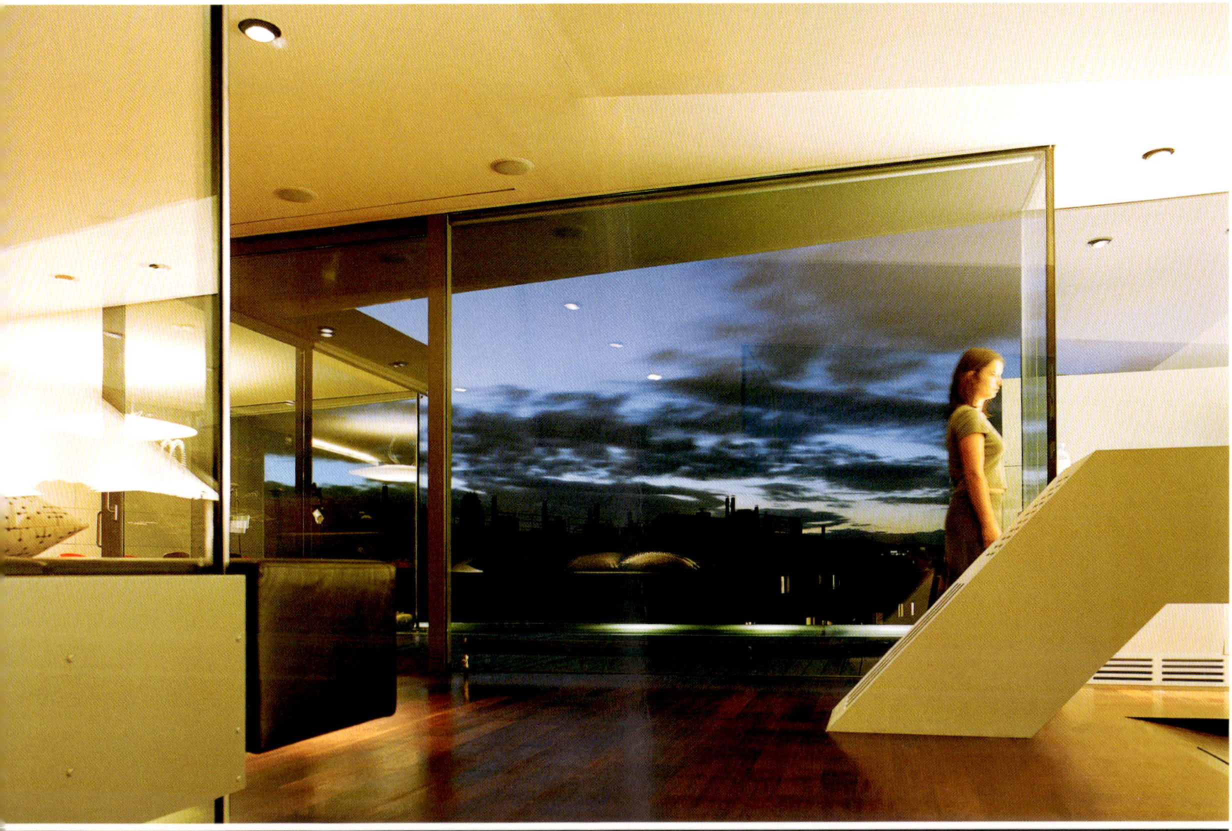
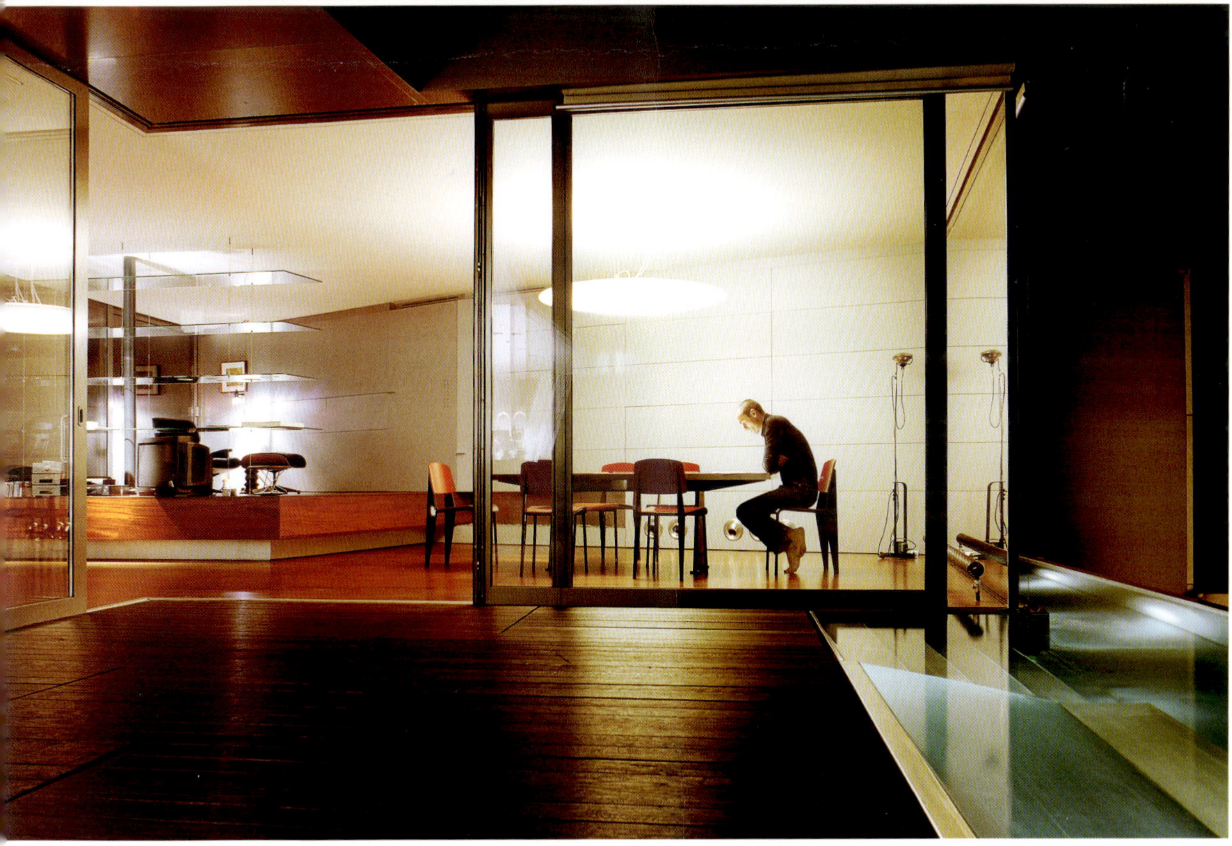

Ray 1, situé dans le paysage des toitures du quatrième arrondissement de Vienne, sur le sommet aplati d'un immeuble de bureaux des années 1960, est issu tout d'abord de ce rapport direct et de la qualité spatiale du lieu. Dans la rencontre du corps statique et de la forme dynamique de l'architecture mobile, l'origine n'est nullement niée, mais au contraire soulignée par cette confrontation. Cette nouvelle construction, issue du rattachement des deux bâtiments adjacents, s'aligne sur les pignons et tient lieu de chaînon manquant dans une certaine mesure. La ligne de démarcation entre le ciel et la terre ne s'entend pas ici comme la séparation entre le toit et le contexte environnant, mais comme une frontière transparente, qui devient elle-même espace de vie. Les entailles et les superpositions, qui créent des zones transparentes et des paysages protégés des deux côtés du bâtiment, permettent d'apprécier la situation dégagée jusqu'à la terrasse où l'on peut déambuler. La peau extérieure revêtue d'une couche d'Alucobond exprime dans l'espace intérieur les différentes valeurs plastiques des diverses zones et niches. L'objectif recherché était de transformer l'enveloppe extérieure du bâtiment en un support de données pour le mobilier, ou encore d'extraire celui-ci de l'architecture : l'espace intérieur se présente comme un loft aux dimensions généreuses, dont les diverses zones fonctionnelles sont définies par des plissements et des différences de hauteur.

Ray 1 está situada entre los tejados del distrito IV de Viena, concretamente sobre el tejado plano de un edificio de oficinas de los años 60. Se genera, ante todo, a partir de este estímulo directo y de la calidad espacial de este lugar. La confrontación de cuerpo estático y forma dinámica de arquitectura en movimiento no desmiente en modo alguno este origen, al contrario, esa coincidencia lo recarga. La nueva construcción se desarrolla a partir de la unión de los dos edificios contiguos continuando la línea frontal y constituye en cierto modo el eslabón perdido. No obstante, la línea de demarcación entre cielo y tierra no se debe entender aquí como separación concluyente entre el tejado y el contexto circundante, sino como límite permeable que se convierte él mismo en espacio habitable. Mediante incisiones y superposiciones se crean zonas transparentes y terrazas protegidas a ambos lados del edificio, que permiten experimentar la estructura abierta hasta llegar al mismo tejado, al que se puede acceder. La piel externa recubierta de Alucobond configura el espacio interior sugiriendo distintas valencias para diferentes zonas y nichos. Aquí el objetivo era convertir la envoltura constructiva en un soporte de datos para los muebles, o mejor dicho, transformar éstos a partir de la arquitectura: el espacio interior está diseñado como un amplio loft cuyas diversas áreas funcionales se definen mediante relieves y diferencias de nivel.

Ray 1, situato su un tetto piano di un edificio a sei piani degli anni '60 con destinazione uffici, si genera innanzi tutto dal diretto contesto e dalla qualità spaziale del luogo. L'incontro tra corpo statico e forma dinamica di un' architettura in movimento, non nega assolutamente l'origine ma invece lo carica. Come continuazione delle linee di colmo, la nuova costruzione collega i due edifici adiacenti e crea così il *missing link*. La linea di demarcazione tra cielo e terra non viene intesa come separazione finale dal tetto e dal contesto circostante ma bensì come confine permeabile che diventa stesso uno spazio vitale. Attraverso incisioni e sovvraposizioni si formano delle aree trasparenti e paesaggi di terrazze protette su tutti i due lati dell' edificio che fanno sperimentare la posizione esposta fino al tetto accessibile. L'involucro esterno di Alucobond modula invece all'interno in maniera plastica differenti valenze spaziali. Lo scopo era di rendere l'involucro dell'edificio un portatore dati dei mobili ovvero di generare quasi tutto l'arredo dall' andamento delle forme architettoniche: lo spazio interno si presenta come loft generoso, le cui varie aree funzionali si definiscono attraverso delle pieghe e differenze di livelli.

APARTMENT HIGH-RISE WIENERBERG
RESIDENTIAL BUILDING | VIENNA
Address: Carl-Appel Straße 7, 1100 Vienna
Client: Mischek, Wohneigentum and Buwog, Vienna
Construction period: 2003-2005
Floor area: 16.600 m²
Photocredits: H. Hurnaus

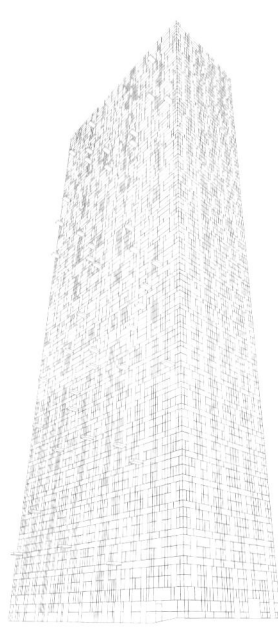

The elegant and simple silhouette of the tower is marked by two contrasting façade typologies which have been determined by their respective orientations. On the south and west sides, the living space is extended by a loggia 1,80 meters deep whose outer glazed wall resembles a delicate curtain, printed with a white bar graphic. The external space functions as a filter and as consciously formulated spatial and visual threshold between inside and outside. By contrast, the north and east parts appear closed. The dark, monolithic impression of the Eternit cladding is heightened by its juxtaposition with freely arranged French windows and individual cantilevered shields and results in an entire, reserved, graphic arrangement. Different apartment types can be connected and thus remain very flexible. The façade design avoids a stereotyped readability of recurring apartment types and – based on the internal demands of the apartments – brings together the internal heterogeneous structure in an overall graphically ordered outer skin.

Die elegante schlichte Silhouette des Turms prägen zwei unterschiedliche Fassadentypologien, die aus der Orientierung des Gebäudes resultieren. Nach Süden und Westen erweitert sich der Wohnraum um eine 1,80 Meter tiefe Loggia, deren äußere Verglasung wie ein filigraner Vorhang wirkt, da er mit einer an Codierungslinien erinnernden Strichgrafik bedruckt ist. Der Freiraum fungiert als Filter und als bewusst artikulierte, räumliche und visuelle Schwelle zwischen innen und außen. Im Gegensatz dazu sind die Nord- und Ostseite verschlossen. Ihre dunkle, monolithische Eternitverkleidung wird von frei angeordneten raumhohen Französischen Fenstern kontrastiert und durch vereinzelt auskragende Schilde akzentuiert, so dass sich eine ganzflächige zurückhaltende, grafische Gliederung ergibt. Verschiedene Wohnungstypen können zusammengeschaltet werden und sind dadurch äußerst flexibel. Die Fassadengestaltung vermeidet eine stereotype Ablesbarkeit sich wiederholender Wohnungsarten und beruhigt, in Übereinstimmung mit den wohnungsinternen Anforderungen, die innere heterogene Struktur in einer ganzheitlich grafisch gegliederten Außenhaut.

L'élégante et fine silhouette de la tour se distingue par le contraste entre les deux typologies de la façade, qui résulte de l'orientation de l'édifice. Au sud et à l'ouest, l'espace habitable se prolonge par une loggia d'une profondeur de 1,80 mètre, dont le vitrage extérieur fait l'effet d'un rideau filigrane, en raison d'une impression pointilliste évocatrice de messages codés. L'espace libre agit tel un filtre et un seuil à l'articulation résolument visuelle et spatiale entre intérieur et extérieur. Les côtés nord et est, en revanche, sont fermés. Leur revêtement monolithique et sombre en Eternit s'oppose à des fenêtres à la française disposées librement et sur toute la hauteur de la pièce, tandis que des panneaux saillants et isolés posent des accents, produisant une articulation graphique et retenue sur toute la surface. Les différents types d'appartements, pouvant être interconnectés, sont de ce fait d'une très grande flexibilité. L'organisation de la façade évite toute lisibilité stéréotypée de types d'appartements se répétant, et tranquillise, conformément aux impératifs internes de ces lieux d'habitation, la structure intérieure hétérogène dans une peau intégralement graphique.

La silueta de la torre, elegante y sencilla, se caracteriza por dos tipologías de fachada en contraste, resultado de la orientación del edificio. En las caras sur y oeste, el espacio vital se amplía mediante balcones de 1,80 metros de profundidad, cuyo acristalamiento exterior grabado con una grafía de puntos que recuerda a un código, produce una impresión de cortina en filigrana. El espacio libre actúa como filtro y como dintel visual y espacial conscientemente articulado entre el interior y el exterior. Por el contrario, las caras norte y este están cerradas. Su oscuro y monolítico revestimiento de eternit contrasta con las exentas ventanas francesas de suelo a techo y está acentuado por planchas en algunos casos voladizas, logrando así una sobria y gráfica distribución a nivel de toda la superficie. Apartamentos de diferentes tipos se pueden conectar entre sí por lo que resultan extraordinariamente flexibles. La configuración de la fachada evita una lectura estereotipada de tipos de vivienda reiterativos y, de acuerdo con las necesidades interiores da serenidad a la heterogénea estructura interna envolviéndola en una piel integral gráficamente dividida.

L'elegante e semplice profilo della torre è caratterizzato da due tipologie di facciata contrastanti che derivano dall'orientamento dell'edificio. A sud e a ovest, l'ambiente abitativo sfocia in una loggia profonda 1,80 metri, la cui vetrata esterna sembra una tenda filigranata, perché vi è stampato un motivo a lineette che ricorda le linee di codificazione. Lo spazio libero funziona da filtro e da soglia, sia a livello spaziale che visivo, tra interno ed esterno. Il lato nord e il lato est invece sono chiusi. Qui, il rivestimento scuro e monolitico in eternit è in contrasto con le alte finestre francesi, distribuite in maniera libera e viene evidenziato da singoli scudi sporgenti; nel complesso, su tutta la superficie si delinea una discreta disposizione grafica. La possibilità di unire vari tipi di appartamento ne garantisce l'estrema flessibilità. L'aspetto della facciata evita la leggibilità stereotipata di appartamenti che si ripetono e coniuga, in accordo con le esigenze dei locali, l'eterogeneità della struttura interna col globale rivestimento esterno a disposizione grafica.

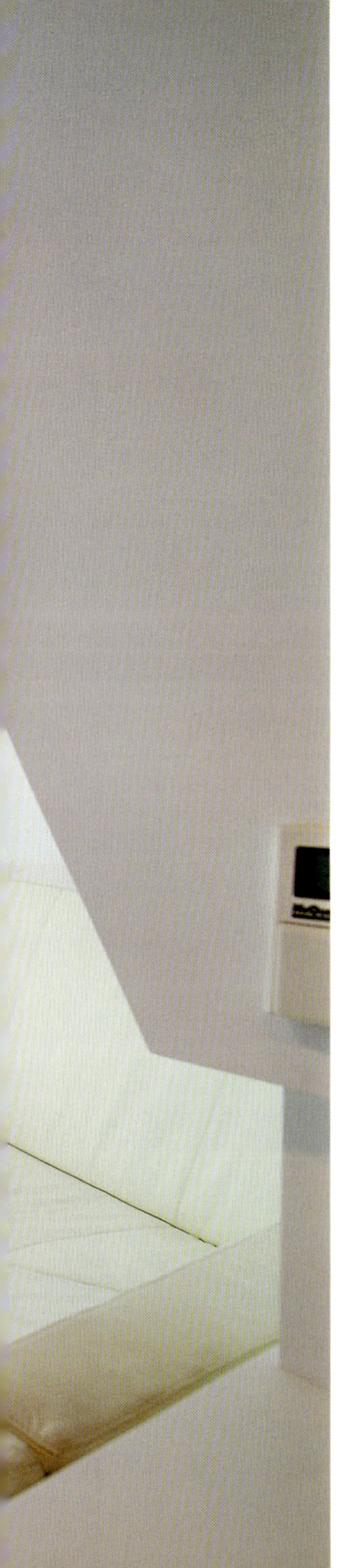

DEEP SURFACE
APARTMENT UNIT 8-II | PHOENIX CITY BEIJING
Exhibition: 1st Architectural Biennial Beijing
Client: CR Land China Resources, Beijing
Construction period: 2004
Floor area: 150 m^2
Photocredits: Biennial Beijing

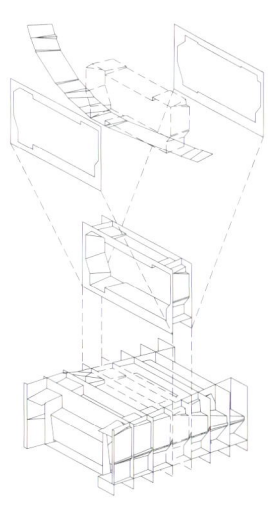

Exhibition: 1st Architectural Biennial Beijing / A5 "Infinite Interior"

In light of China's rapidly growing architectural development, it seems obvious to lend spatial expression to the fast pace and dynamism of this process. The uninterrupted change of Beijing's cityscape has taken on an almost virtual character, one that nevertheless also adheres to the reality of the construction industry. The contrast between such seemingly irreconcilable concepts as speed and contemplation or virtuality and reality forms the basis of this design.

A multiply convoluted crystalline "furniture landscape" which consistently recognizes floors, ceiling, and walls as equal parameters, makes the apartment being conceived as a flowing spatial continuum. The given spatial layout is undermined, though not actually negated, by this "architecture of transition". The classical linear spatial boundaries expand, unfold themselves and become perceptible as great convolutions. Converging here is the tensely stark contrast of an architecture that on the one hand possesses a strong spatial presence in its expressiveness and dynamism, while on the other appearing as an unobtrusive, diffusely-lit spatial configuration.

Ausstellung: 1st Architectural Biennial Beijing / A5 „Infinite Interior"

Vor dem Hintergrund der rasanten Architekturentwicklung Chinas scheint es nahe liegend, der Schnelligkeit und Dynamik dieses Prozesses auch räumlich Ausdruck zu verleihen. Die kontinuierliche Veränderung des Pekinger Stadtbildes hat einen nahezu virtuellen Charakter, der nichtsdestotrotz dem Realitätsbezug der Baubranche Rechnung trägt. Das Aufeinandertreffen solcher, auf den ersten Blick scheinbarer Gegensätze wie Geschwindigkeit und Kontemplation oder Virtualität und Realität bildet die Entwurfsgrundlage.

Eine gefaltete, kristalline „Möbellandschaft", die Boden, Decke und Wände gleichwertig einbezieht, lässt das Apartment als fließendes räumliches Kontinuum erscheinen. Die vorgegebene Raumaufteilung wird durch diese „Architektur des Übergangs" unterlaufen, ohne sie tatsächlich zu verleugnen. Die klassischen linearen Raumbegrenzungen dehnen sich aus und werden als raumgreifende Faltungen erlebbar. Hier vereint sich der spannungsvolle Gegensatz einer Architektur, die einerseits in ihrer Expressivität und Dynamik räumlich stark präsent ist und andererseits als diffus lichte Raumkonfiguration in Erscheinung tritt.

Exposition: 1st Architectural Biennial Beijing / A5 « Infinite Interior »

Face au développement fulgurant de la Chine, il semble logique de donner une expression spatiale à la rapidité et à la dynamique de ce processus. La modification incessante du paysage urbain de Pékin possède un caractère presque virtuel, qui ne tient pas moins compte du réalisme du secteur immobilier. Le projet se fonde sur la rencontre de ce qui paraît à première vue des antithèses, telles que vitesse et contemplation ou virtualité et réalité. Un « paysage mobilier » plissé et cristallin, qui englobe tant les sols et les plafonds que les murs, donne à l'appartement l'aspect d'un continuum spatial fluide. La distribution spécifiée des pièces se fonde sur cette « architecture de la transition », sans réellement la nier. Les limites linéaires classiques s'étendent et se perçoivent en tant que plissements qui s'emparent de l'espace. Une architecture fortement présente dans son expressivité et sa dynamique s'oppose ici, en toute harmonie, avec sa configuration spatiale lâche et diffuse.

Exposición: 1st Architectural Biennial Beijing / A5 "Infinite Interior"

En vista de la rasante evolución que está experimentando la arquitectura en China parece obvio dar también una expresión espacial a la velocidad y dinámica de este proceso. La imagen urbana de Pekín está sometida a un cambio continuo que tiene un carácter casi virtual sin perder por ello el contacto con la realidad de la rama de la construcción. La convergencia de conceptos, sólo a primera vista opuestos, como velocidad y contemplación o virtualidad y realidad, constituye la base del diseño. Un "paisaje mobiliario" cristalino y sinuoso que implica por igual suelos, techos y paredes, proporciona al apartamento una sensación de continua fluidez espacial. Esta "arquitectura de transición" socava la distribución espacial prescrita, pero sin negarla realmente. Los clásicos límites lineales del espacio se expanden y se hacen perceptibles como grandes relieves. Aquí converge el contraste lleno de tensión de una arquitectura que por una parte posee una fuerte presencia espacial en su expresividad y dinámica y por otra, aparece como una configuración espacial difusamente diáfana.

Mostra: 1st Architectural Biennial Beijing / A5 "Infinite Interior"

Sullo sfondo del celere sviluppo architettonico cinese, sembra logico conferire alla velocità e alla dinamicità di questo processo anche un'espressione spaziale. Il cambiamento continuo dell'aspetto della città di Pechino ha un carattere quasi virtuale che, nonostante tutto, tiene conto del riferimento alla realtà dell'edilizia. L'incontro di tali, almeno a prima vista apparenti opposti, come velocità e contemplazione o virtualità e realtà, rappresenta la base del progetto. Un "paesaggio di mobili", ripiegato e cristallino che include equiparabilmente pavimento, soffitto e pareti, fa apparire l'appartamento come un continuum spaziale e fluido. La suddivisione prescritta delle stanze è minata da questa "architettura di passaggio", senza rinnegarla realmente. I classici margini lineari degli spazi si ampliano e diventano riconoscibili come pieghe estese nello spazio. In questo modo si riconcilia il contrasto avvincente di un'architettura che, da un lato è molto presente nello spazio con la sua espressività e dinamicità, dall'altro si manifesta come configurazione spaziale caratterizzata da luce soffusa.

KALLCO CITY LOFTS
RESIDENTIAL BUILDING WITH OFFICES
AND A KINDERGARTEN | VIENNA
Address: Hertha-Firnberg-Straße 10, 1100 Vienna
Client: Kallco Bauträger GmbH, Vienna
Construction period: 2002-2004
Floor area: 5.313 m^2
Photocredits: H. Hurnaus

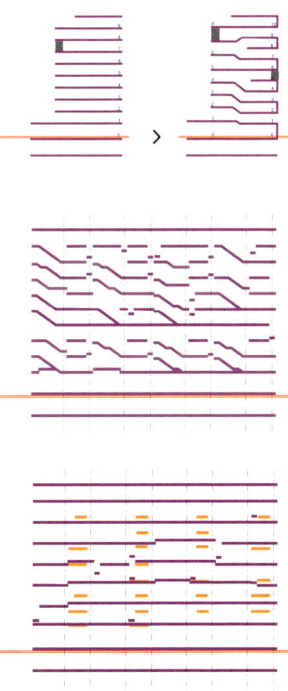

The project was first of all based on the demands for a kindergarten, apartments, offices and additional working spaces within an eight-story building and a floor height of 2,50 meters. Conditions referred to in their essence, were subject to variation in order to enable a new, quality driven and flexible kind of living. In place of the simple stacking of identical layers, the design uses interlocking floors to create spaces of differing heights. The floor height of the living rooms situated in the south, was raised up to 3,40 meters while the northern facing bedrooms and utility rooms have been lowered. This cogging of different room heights, combined with a complex access system, has resulted in an unusual variety of different styles of apartments. Detached from the living space, there are individual northern facing office or utility boxes with a glass front for rent. Together with the L-shaped bedroom windows, they create a dynamic façade which reflects the complex internal structure of the building. The south facing front received a balcony that spans across the entire façade with a pre-fronted black parapet which quotes the motif of the internal meandering pathways.

Das Projekt basierte zunächst auf den Forderungen nach einem Kindertagesheim, Wohnungen, Büros und zusätzlichen Arbeitsraumangeboten bei acht Geschossen und einer Raumhöhe von 2,50 Meter. Bedingungen, die ihrem Wesen nach zitiert, aber durchaus variiert wurden, um ein spezifisches neues, qualitätsvolles und variables Wohnen zu ermöglichen. Nicht das bloße Aufeinanderschichten gleicher Ebenen ohne inneren Zusammenhang war das Ziel, sondern ein räumliches Geflecht, das sich als differenzierte Wohn- und Arbeitswelt herausbildet.

Die im Süden liegenden Wohnräume wurden auf 3,40 Meter erhöht, während die dem Norden zugewandten Schlaf- und Hobbyräume niedriger ausgebildet sind. Durch die Verzahnung der unterschiedlichen Raumhöhen entstand in Verbindung mit einem komplexen Erschließungssystem eine ungewöhnliche Vielfalt von Wohnungstypen. Auf der Nordseite befinden sich, von den Wohnungen abgekoppelte, individuell anmietbare, verglaste Büro- oder Hobbyboxen, die, im Wechselspiel mit den L-förmigen Fenstern der Schlafräume, ein dynamisches Fassadenbild entstehen lassen, das die komplexe innere Verschachtelung abbildet. Die Südfassade erhielt eine durchgehende Balkonschicht mit einem vorgelagerten schwarzen Brüstungsband, das das Motiv des Gangmäanders im Inneren zitiert.

Le projet devait tout d'abord répondre à divers impératifs : une crèche, des appartements, bureaux et locaux commerciaux supplémentaires, le tout sur huit étages et pour une hauteur sous plafond de 2,50 mètres. Des conditions qui ont été respectées mais avec des variantes notables, afin de pouvoir associer un habitat réellement nouveau à une qualité élevée et à une grande variabilité. L'objet n'était pas d'empiler simplement différentes strates sans cohésion interne, mais de créer un réseau spatial distinguant entre zones d'habitation et aires de travail.

La hauteur sous plafond des pièces à vivre, orientées au sud, a été portée à 3,40 mètres, les chambres et les pièces réservées aux loisirs, côté nord, étant plus basses de plafond. L'indentation des différentes hauteurs sous plafond, liée à un système complexe d'ouvertures, a autorisé une grande diversité de types d'appartements. Côté nord se trouvent les cubes destinés aux bureaux et aux loisirs, loués séparément, qui sont détachés des appartements et, qui, en alternant avec les fenêtres en L des chambres, créent une façade dynamique reproduisant la complexité des imbrications intérieures. La façade sud est dotée d'un balcon continu muni d'un parapet noir qui cite le méandre des couloirs à l'intérieur.

El proyecto tenía ante todo que ajustarse a las necesidades de una guardería, viviendas, oficinas y otros locales comerciales complementarios, todo repartido en ocho pisos y con techos de 2,50 metros de altura. Estas condiciones sirvieron de referencia en lo esencial, pero se variaron para hacer posible un modo de vida específico con más calidad y diversidad. El objetivo no era superponer pisos iguales sin conexión interior, sino crear un entramado espacial como universo diferenciado para vivir y trabajar.

En las estancias orientadas al sur se elevaron los techos hasta 3,40 metros, mientras que en las del norte, destinadas a dormitorios y cuartos de ocio se construyeron más bajos. El engranaje de alturas distintas unido a un complejo sistema de infraestructura dio lugar a una inusitada variedad de tipos de vivienda. En la parte norte y desacopladas de las viviendas, hay cajas individuales cubiertas de cristal que se pueden alquilar como oficinas y cuartos de ocio y, que en alternancia con las ventanas en forma de L de los dormitorios, crean una fachada dinámica, reflejo del complejo intríngulis del interior. La fachada sur está cubierta por una línea continua de balcones cuya balaustrada antepuesta forma una banda negra que hace referencia al meandro interno de corredores.

Il progetto si basava inizialmente sull'esigenza di un asilo nido, di appartamenti, di uffici e di spazi lavorativi addizionali su otto piani e un'altezza dei vani di 2,50 metri. Condizioni che furono rispettate, ma anche assolutamente variate, per consentire un nuovo specifico modo di abitare d'alta qualità e variabilità. Lo scopo non era di accatastare semplicemente piani uguali senza una relazione interna, quanto creare un intreccio dello spazio che si presentasse come un mondo abitativo e lavorativo differenziato.

I locali della zona giorno sul lato sud furono rialzati a 3,40 metri, mentre le stanze da letto e da hobby rivolte a nord furono realizzate più basse. Attraverso la concatenazione di ambienti di diverse dimensioni e il macchinoso sistema di accesso, si è creata una varietà insolita di tipi di appartamenti. Sul lato nord, staccati dalle abitazioni, si trovano uffici e box-hobby a vetrate che possono essere affittati individualmente; queste vetrate, insieme alle finestre a L delle stanze da letto, creano una facciata a effetto dinamico che riproduce il complesso concatenamento dell'interno. La facciata a sud presenta uno strato continuo di balconi con un, anteposta balaustra a fascia nera che riprende il motivo del meandro di corridoi all' interno.

GLOBAL HEADQUARTERS SANDOZ, NOVARTIS COMPANY
INTERIOR DESIGN | VIENNA
Address: Wagramer Strasse 19, 1220 Vienna
Client: BC Biochemie Pharma GmbH, Ismaning
Construction period: 2002-2003
Floor area: 2.900 m^2
Photocredits: R. Steiner

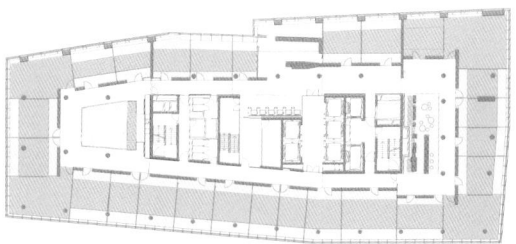

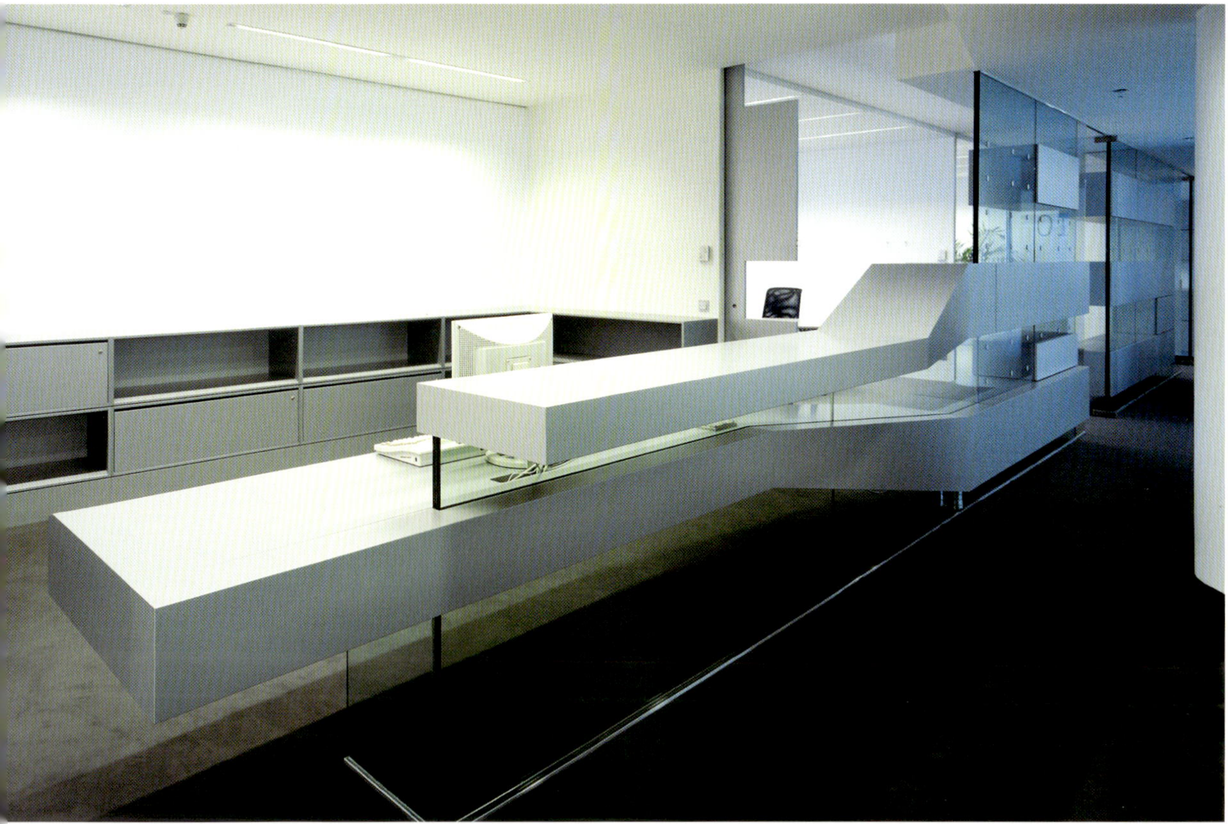

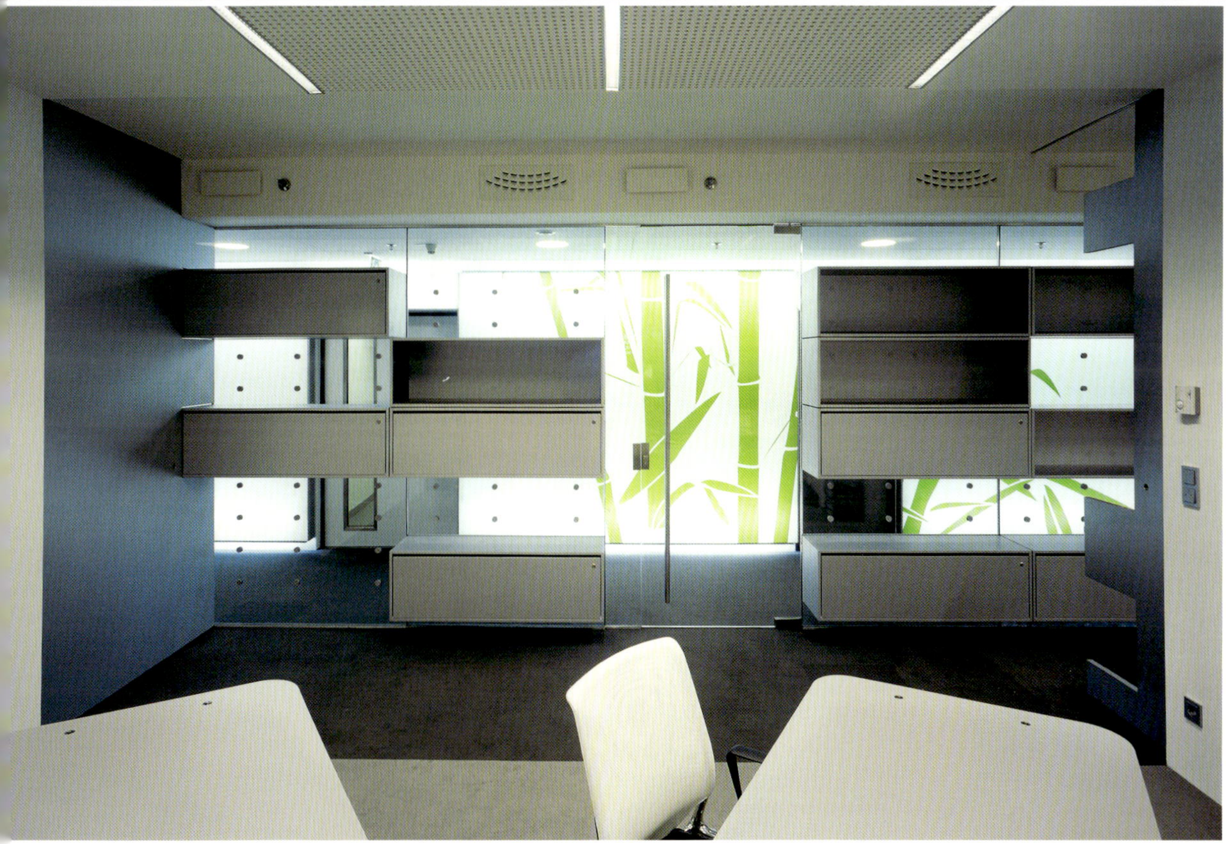

The flexible shelf system NovaMobile, especially developed for Novartis, is based on the spatial segmentation of access and office space. Yet at the same time it forms zones of differing density – depending on the requirements and communication values of each given place. Different module types (shelving units, open and closed cabinets) – fixed to supporting glass walls that reach all the way to the ceiling – enable the parallel formulation of closed areas, semitransparent as well as absolute transparent zones in the different communication and work spaces. The different options can be assembled on site in any combination according to the clients' needs. NovaMobile serves as a space-defining element and visual guideline. The interplay between the pattern principle of the linear module based system and the facing backlit wall with a bamboo print creates a suspenseful hallway area whose impact goes beyond the purely functional aspect.

Das speziell für Novartis entwickelte flexible Regalsystem NovaMobile basiert auf der räumlichen Trennung von Erschließungszonen und Büroräumen, bildet dabei jedoch – je nach Anforderung und Kommunikationsgehalt des jeweiligen Ortes – unterschiedlich dichte Bereiche aus. Durch die Kombination verschiedener Modultypen (Regalfächer, offene und geschlossene Kästen), die an raumhohen tragenden Glaswänden fixiert werden, entstehen zugleich abgeschlossene Bereiche, semi-transparente und vollkommen durchsichtige Zonen, die durch eine variable Montage vor Ort direkt auf die Mitarbeiterwünsche zugeschnitten werden können. NovaMobile ist raumbildendes Element und visuelles Wegeleitsystem. Im Zusammenspiel vom Patternprinzip des linearen Modulsystems und der mit einer Bambusgrafik bedruckten, gegenüber angeordneten Leuchtwand, wird der Gangbereich zu einem spannungsvollen Ort, der über den rein funktionalen Aspekt hinausgeht.

Le système d'étagères flexible NovaMobile conçu spécialement pour Novartis se fonde sur la séparation spatiale entre aires ouvertes et espaces de bureaux, mais permet aussi de délimiter – selon les impératifs et le degré de communication du lieu en question – des zones de densité variable. La combinaison de divers types de modules (tiroirs, boîtes ouvertes et fermées), fixés sur des parois vitrées faisant toute la hauteur de la pièce, permet de créer tant des zones fermées que semi-transparentes ou transparentes, qui, compte tenu des diverses possibilités de montage sur site, répondent directement aux souhaits des salariés. NovaMobile est un élément qui structure l'espace et un réseau de communication visuel. Le couloir, grâce à l'interaction entre les motifs du système modulaire linéaire et la paroi lumineuse qui lui fait face, imprimée d'un graphisme faisant appel au bambou, devient un lieu saisissant qui va au-delà de l'aspect purement fonctionnel.

El sistema de estanterías flexible especialmente diseñado para Novartis con el nombre de NovaMobile está destinado fundamentalmente a la separación espacial de zonas de acceso y despachos y no obstante, da lugar a áreas de diferente densidad según las necesidades y el grado de accesibilidad del lugar concreto. Combinando módulos de diferentes tipos (estantes, cajones abiertos y cerrados) que se fijan a paneles de cristal cuya superficie se extiende de suelo a techo, se crean espacios cerrados y zonas transparentes o semitransparentes. Gracias a su montaje variable se pueden adaptar in situ según las necesidades de los empleados. NovaMobile es simultáneamente elemento distribuidor y sistema indicador visual. El esquemático sistema modular y lineal se enfrenta cara a cara con una pared luminosa grabada con motivos de bambú. La interacción de ambos convierte el pasillo en un lugar estimulante que rebasa el mero aspecto funcional.

Il sistema flessibile di scaffali NovaMobile, sviluppato appositamente per Novartis, si basa sulla divisione spaziale di zone di accesso ed uffici, crea però, a seconda delle esigenze e del contenuto comunicativo di ogni luogo, ambienti di diversa densità. Attraverso la combinazione di differenti tipi di moduli (mensole, casse aperte o chiuse), da fissare a pareti portanti di vetro alte quanto la stanza stessa, si formano contemporaneamente spazi chiusi, zone semitrasparenti e trasparenti che possono essere rese delle dimensioni desiderate grazie al montaggio variabile sul posto. NovaMobile è un elemento per la creazione di spazi e una guida visuale di percorsi. Nel gioco d'insieme del principio dei *pattern* del sistema lineare e modulare e della parete luminosa con stampato un motivo di bambù posta di fronte, il corridoio diviene un luogo avvincente che va oltre l'aspetto puramente funzionale.

DELUGAN MEISSL ASSOCIATED ARCHITECTS
inTENSE repose

inTENSE repose 2006/2007
Touring Exhibition: Delugan Meissl Associated Architects
Implementation in cooperation with Zumtobel and Aedes
Photocredits: Delugan Meissl, F. Leutner

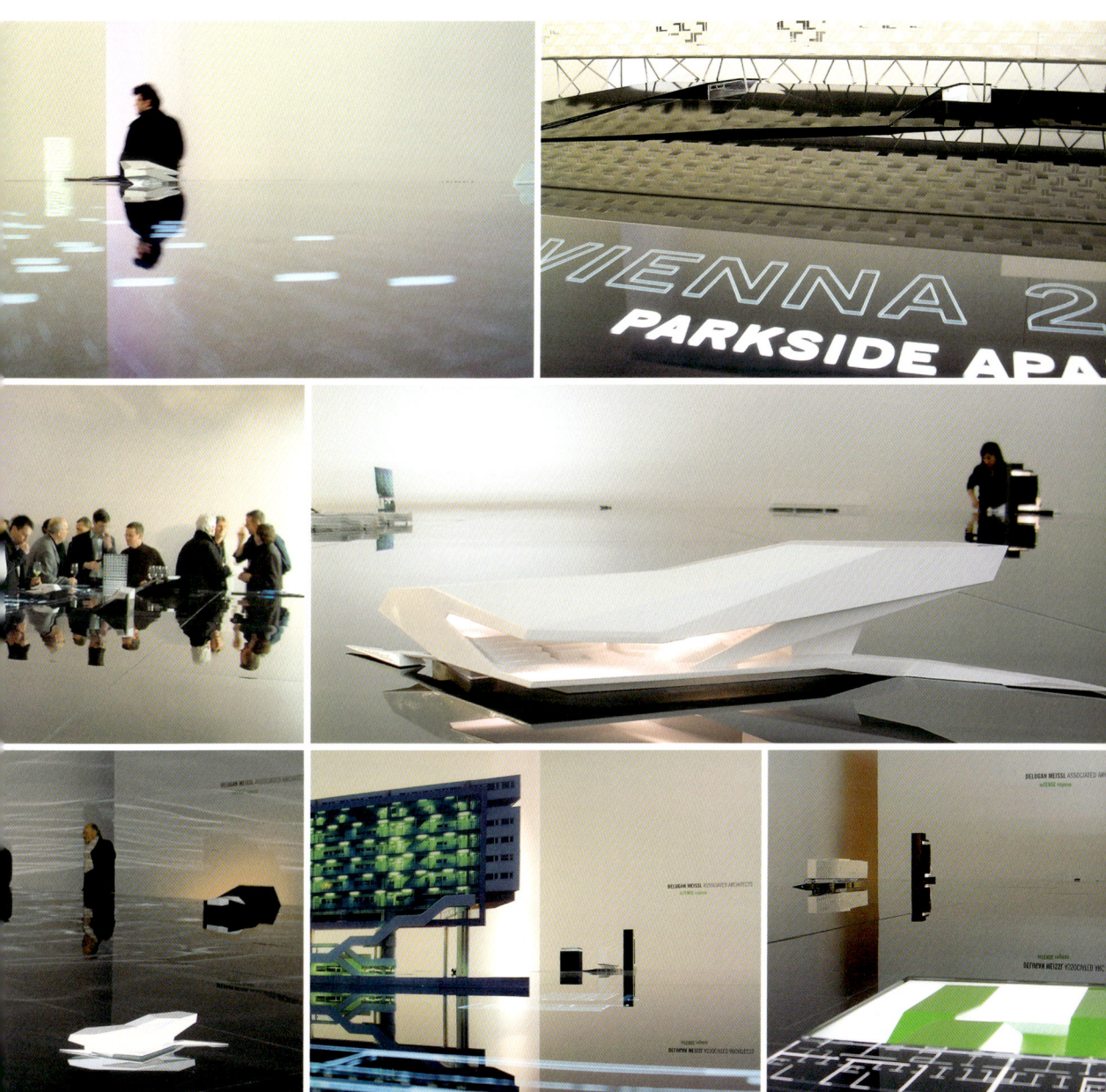

Delugan Meissl Associated Architects show a selection of their projects from the last 13 years. Embedded in the contradictory field of processes and layering, different genres and architectural approaches will be presented with 19 projects and exhibited in a dialogue manner on a big board.

The fundamental approach, typical of the Viennese office, of creating space out of the effectual architectural relationship and the specific environment is inverted: the concept reacts to different, already existent show rooms which by means of an "implant" are not only precisely defined but also filled with suspense. The big board is presented in the form of a an expansive black monolith and consists of modules that can be configured anew depending on their location. The horizontal surface acts as a display system. Printed drawings are lit from below, special spot lights light up embedded models and the pressing of any one of a number of button has a variety of photos, animations and visualisations appear on integrated monitors. This way the visitor is free to choose the level of interaction with architecture. At the same time we have an expansive installation which contrasts the reduced semiotics of form of the exhibited item with its reflecting surface against the background of the interplay between man, architecture and light.

The exhibition has been opened in March 2006 in Dornbirn and will continue until the end of the year in the following cities: Glasgow, London, Manchester, Hamburg, Amsterdam, Berlin. During 2007 the travelling exhibition will take place in: Stuttgart, Vienna, Brussels, Zurich, Lemgo, New York and Tokyo.

Delugan Meissl Associated Architects zeigen einen Querschnitt ihrer architektonischen Arbeiten der vergangenen 13 Jahre. Im Spannungsfeld unterschiedlicher Prozesse und Schichtungen werden die verschiedenen Genres und differenziert offenen Zugänge zur Architektur anhand von 19 Projekten präsentiert und auf einer großen Tafel in Dialog gestellt.

Der grundsätzliche, für das Wiener Büro typische Zugang, aus dem spezifischen Umfeld und architektonischen Wirkungszusammenhang, Raum zu schaffen, wird hier umgekehrt: Das Konzept reagiert auf unterschiedliche, bestehende Ausstellungsräume, die über ein „Implantat" nicht nur genauestens definiert, sondern auch spannungsvoll aufgeladen werden. Die große Tafel in Form eines raumgreifenden, schwarzen Monoliths besteht aus Modulen, die je nach Ort neu konfiguriert werden können. Die horizontale Oberfläche wird als Displaysystem ausgebildet. Aufgedruckte Zeichnungen werden von unten beleuchtet, eingelassene Modelle über gezielte Spots inszeniert und Fotos, Animationen und Visualisierungen per Knopfdruck auf integrierten Bildschirmen sichtbar. Auf diese Weise kann die Intensität der Auseinandersetzung mit der Architektur vom Besucher frei gewählt werden. Gleichzeitig entsteht eine räumlich großflächige Installation, die die reduzierte Formensprache des Ausstellungsmöbels mit dessen reflektierender Oberfläche im Wechselspiel von Mensch, Architektur und Licht in Kontrast setzt.

Die Wanderausstellung wurde im März 2006 in Dornbirn im Zumtobel Lichtforum eröffnet und wird bis Ende des Jahres in Glasgow, London, Manchester, Hamburg, Amsterdam, Berlin und im Laufe von 2007 in Stuttgart, Wien, Brüssel, Zürich, Lemgo, New York und Tokyo zu sehen sein.

Le studio Delugan Meissl Associated Architects présente une coupe transversale de ses travaux architecturaux des 13 dernières années. À travers les antagonismes entre les divers processus et stratifications, le visiteur découvre les différents genres et accède à l'architecture à l'aide de 19 projets ouverts au débat sur un grand panneau.

L'entrée typique prônée par le studio viennois qui crée un espace à partir de l'environnement spécifique et de son rapport à l'effet architectonique, se trouve ici inversée : le concept réagit à différentes salles d'exposition existantes, définies non seulement avec une extrême précision par un « implant », mais aussi chargées de tensions. Le grand panneau qui prend la forme d'un monolithe noir accapareur d'espace, se compose de modules pouvant être reconfigurés en fonction du lieu. La surface horizontale constitue un système d'affichage. Les dessins imprimés sont éclairés par en dessous, les maquettes mises en scène par des spots précis et, pour voir les photographies, les animations et les visuels, il suffit d'appuyer sur le bouton d'un écran intégré. Le visiteur peut ainsi choisir librement l'intensité de sa découverte architecturale. Simultanément se crée une installation qui s'empare d'une grande surface et établit un contraste entre le répertoire réduit du meuble d'exposition et sa surface réfléchissante, dans l'interaction entre homme, architecture et lumière.

L'exposition ambulante, inaugurée en mars 2006 à Dornbirn au Zumtobel Lichtforum, se rendra d'ici la fin de l'année à Glasgow, Londres, Manchester, Hambourg, Amsterdam, Berlin, puis, en 2007, à Stuttgart, Vienne, Bruxelles, Zurich, Lemgo, New York et Tokyo.

Delugan Meissl Associated Architects muestran un perfil de sus trabajos arquitectónicos de los últimos 13 años. En el campo de tensión de diferentes procesos y estratificaciones, los distintos géneros y los modos abiertos y diferenciados de acceder a la arquitectura se presentan en base a 19 proyectos y se abren al dialogo sobre un gran tablero.

Aquí se da la vuelta al procedimiento fundamental y típico del despacho vienés, que es crear espacio a partir de un entorno específico y de un estímulo arquitectónico: el concepto responde a diferentes salas de exposición ya existentes, que mediante un "implante" no sólo se definen con la mayor exactitud, sino que también se cargan de tensión. El gran tablero en forma de voluminoso monolito negro se compone de módulos que se pueden volver a configurar según el lugar. La superficie horizontal se convierte en sistema visualizador. Planos impresos se iluminan desde abajo, focos de luz selectivos ponen en escena maquetas empotradas y apretando un botón aparecen fotos, animaciones y visualizaciones sobre pantallas (integradas). De este modo, el visitante puede elegir libremente con que intensidad desea enfrentarse a la arquitectura. Simultáneamente se crea una gran instalación espacial que hace contrastar el reducido lenguaje de formas del mobiliario expositor con su superficie reflectante en un juego de alternancia de ser humano, arquitectura y luz.

La exposición se inauguró en marzo de 2006 en el Zumtobel Lichtforum de Dornbirn y hasta finales de año se verá en Glasgow, Londres, Manchester, Hamburgo, Ámsterdam y Berlín, y a lo largo de 2007 en Stuttgart, Viena, Bruselas, Zúrich, Lemgo, Nueva York y Tokio.

Delugan Meissl Associated Architects mostrano una rassegna dei loro lavori architettonici degli ultimi 13 anni. 19 progetti, esposti su una grande tavola, presentano i vari generi e i differenti liberi approcci all'architettura nella tensione di diversi processi e stratificazioni.

Il sostanziale approccio, tipico dello studio viennese, di generare lo spazio partendo dall'ambiente specifico e dal contesto d'azione architettonico viene qui capovolto. Il progetto reagisce alle diverse sale d'esposizione esistenti, le quali non solo vengono esattamente definite da un "trapianto", ma anche caricate di energia. La grande tavola, costituita da un enorme monolito nero, è composta di moduli che possono essere configurati in modi diversi a seconda del luogo. La superficie orizzontale serve come sistema d'esposizione. I disegni stampati sono illuminati dal basso, i modelli incassati sono messi in scena da spot mirati, le foto, le animazioni e le visualizzazioni sono da ammirare su schermi integrati. In questo modo il visitatore stesso stabilisce l'intensità della sua discussione con l'architettura. Allo stesso tempo si crea un'istallazione estesa nello spazio, che mette in contrasto il linguaggio ridotto del mobile d'esposizione con la sua superficie riflettente, nel gioco alterno di uomo, architettura e luce.

La mostra itinerante è stata inaugurata nel marzo 2006 a Dornbirn nel Lichtforum Zumtobel. Sarà possibile visitarla fino alla fine dell'anno a Glasgow, Londra, Manchester, Amburgo, Amsterdam, Berlino e nel corso del 2007 a Stoccarda, Vienna, Bruxelles, Zurigo, Lemgo, New York e Tokyo.

HOUSE RT
SINGLE FAMILY HOUSE | AUSTRIA
Client: Private
Construction period: 2004-2005
Site area: 2.791 m^2
Floor area: 554 m^2
Photocredits: H. Hurnaus

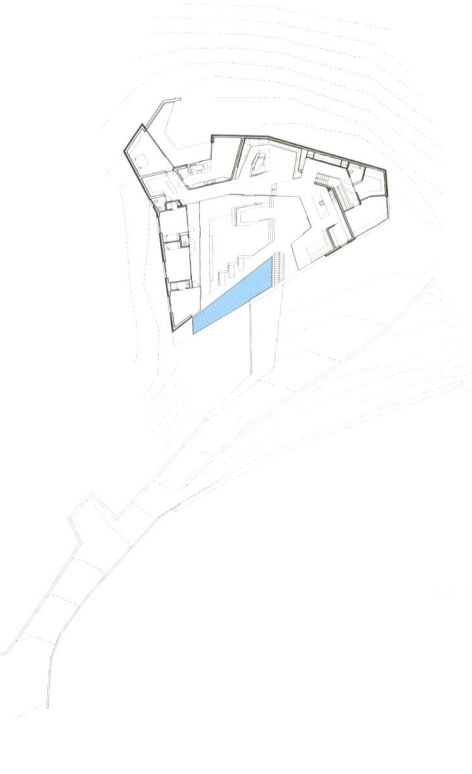

The site's sloping terrain at the edge of the woods presents an impressive panoramic view of the valley and the surrounding mountain landscape is the design's point of departure: the house is placed at the center of a clearing and conceived as an atrium structure which incorporates itself cautiously into its surroundings. The atrium enables a conclusive circulating organization of the internal relations that offer the inhabitants defined yet open options for retreat, as well as spectacular sweeping views and ideal opportunities for spending time outdoors. Through its sculptural form and the black crack pattern of the façade the house positions itself boldly in the charged interaction with nature.

The architects designed nearly all furniture: the living area with the big chimney in form of a central sculpture, around which the seating area is organized, the bedrooms or the kitchen. The bath and wellness area received special attention in that it incorporates an inset bath, spacious furnishings, relaxation areas, washing facilities, storage spaces and multimedia walls.

Die eindrucksvolle Hanglage des Grundstücks am Waldrand, mit einem großartigen Panoramablick ins Tal und die umliegende Berglandschaft, war der Ausgangspunkt für den Entwurf des Einfamilienhauses. Das Gebäude wurde ins Zentrum der Lichtung gerückt und als Atriumhaus konzipiert, welches sich behutsam in die spezifische Landschaft einfügt. Das Atrium ermöglicht eine schlüssige umlaufende Organisation der internen Zusammenhänge, welche den Bewohnern eindeutig definierte, aber dennoch offene Rückzugsmöglichkeiten sowie, bei bester Weitsicht, eine großzügige außenräumliche Aufenthaltsqualität bietet. Durch die körperhafte Formgebung und das schwarze *crack pattern* der Fassade positioniert sich das Wohnhaus im spannungsvollen Aufeinandertreffen mit der Natur selbstbewusst im Kontext der Topographie.

Nahezu alle Möbel wurden von den Architekten speziell entwickelt: Sei es der Wohnbereich mit dem großen, als zentrale Skulptur ausgebildeten Kamin, um den herum sich die Sitzlandschaft organisiert, die Schlafräume oder die Küche. Besondere Aufmerksamkeit galt zudem der Gestaltung des Bad- und Wellnessbereiches, der – neben einer in den Boden eingelassenen Badewanne – ein raumgreifendes Möbel, Ruhezonen, Waschgelegenheiten, Ablageflächen und Multimediawände in sich birgt.

La conception de cette maison familiale se fonde sur l'impressionnante situation en pente du terrain, à la lisière d'une forêt, d'où une vue panoramique fabuleuse sur la vallée et les montagnes environnantes. Placée au centre d'une clairière, elle est disposée autour d'un atrium et s'insère avec circonspection dans le paysage spécifique. L'atrium autorise une organisation résolument circulaire des rapports internes. Ceux-ci offrent aux habitants des possibilités de retraite bien définies et néanmoins ouvertes, de même que, avec des vues optimisées, une remarquable qualité de séjour extérieur. Par le façonnage sculptural et le *crack pattern* noir de la façade, la maison d'habitation fait montre d'assurance dans sa rencontre riche de tensions avec la nature dans le contexte de la topographie.

Les architectes ont conçu spécialement presque tous les meubles, qu'il s'agisse de ceux des chambres, de la cuisine ou de la salle de séjour avec la grande cheminée pensée comme une statue centrale, autour de laquelle s'organisent les sièges. Une attention particulière a été accordée à l'aménagement des salles d'eau et de remise en forme, qui renferment, à côté d'une baignoire encastrée dans le sol, des meubles, des coins repos, des équipements de toilettes, des zones de rangement et des murs multimédias.

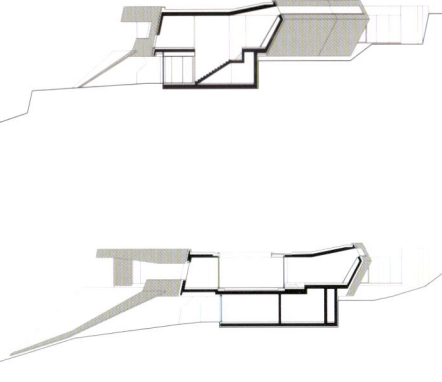

El impresionante terreno en pendiente situado en el lindero del bosque y por encima de la ciudad próxima, así como la magnífica vista del valle y de las montañas circundantes constituyeron el punto de partida para el diseño de la casa unifamiliar. El edificio se emplazó en el centro del claro y se concibió como una casa-atrio, que se incorpora cuidadosamente al paisaje específico. El atrio permite una organización circundante y lógica de las conexiones internas. Éstas ofrecen a los habitantes posibilidades de retiro claramente definidas y no obstante abiertas, así como una gran calidad de vida exterior con el mejor de los panoramas. Su escultural configuración y la fachada negra de *crack pattern* permiten que la casa, en tensa confrontación con la naturaleza, tome posición de manera consciente en el contexto de la topografía.

Casi todos los muebles fueron diseñados especialmente por los propios arquitectos: tanto en la zona de estar con una gran chimenea concebida como escultura central, en torno a la cual se organiza el conjunto de asientos, como en el dormitorio o en la cocina. Se dedicó especial atención a la disposición de la zona de baño y wellness, que además de una bañera integrada en el suelo, alberga un gran mueble, zonas de descanso, lavabos, superficies de repisa y paredes multimedia.

La posizione inclinata di grande effetto del terreno al margine di un bosco, un panorama magnifico sulla valle e il paesaggio montano circostante sono stati il punto di partenza per la progettazione della casa unifamiliare. L'edificio è stato piazzato al centro della radura e concepito come una casa atrio, che si inserisce con rispetto nel paesaggio. L'atrio rende possibile un'organizzazione circolare convincente dei collegamenti interni. Questi ultimi offrono agli inquilini possibilità di ritiro chiaramente definite, ma nondimeno aperte, e una qualità di soggiorno da spazio esterno. Grazie alla forma a scultura e al *crack pattern* nero della facciata, l'edificio si erge fiero in questo avvincente confronto con la natura, sullo sfondo del contesto topografico.

Gli architetti hanno creato quasi tutti i mobili su misura: sia il soggiorno con il grande caminetto, progettato come scultura centrale intorno al quale si organizza lo spazio per sedersi, sia le camere da letto, sia la cucina. Particolare attenzione è stata dedicata all'arredamento di bagno e zona wellness, che, oltre a una vasca da bagno incassata nel pavimento, comprende un mobile di grandi misure, luoghi di riposo, possibilità di lavarsi, superfici di appoggio e pareti multimediali.

APARTMENTS PALTRAMPLATZ
RESIDENTIAL BUILDING | VIENNA
Address: Carl-Appel Straße 7, 1100 Vienna
Client: Neues Leben, Vienna
Construction period: 2001-2002
Site area: 387 m^2
Floor area: 1.550 m^2
Photocredits: M. Spiluttini, Delugan Meissl

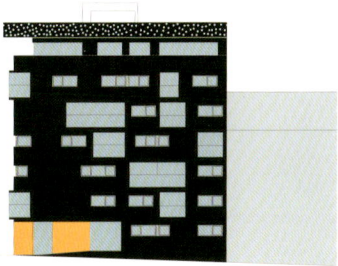

The residential building leaves an indelible mark on the densely packed landscape of Gründerzeit buildings, amidst which it stands out as a sharply delineated, monolithic, matte black cube whose jutting, irregularly arranged, bright loggias charge the entire structure by introducing an element of contrast. These floor-to-ceiling glazed loggias which interact with the elegant mosaic of freely-arranged, dark Eternit slabs, function as extensions of the apartments into the green space of the park, at the same time serving as the central element determining the appearance of the façade. The extremely cantilevered, perforated roof construction provides a counterweight to the severity of this corner building and caps its upper edge with a dynamic gesture. The rooftop terrace is open to all and its sauna and relaxation zones offer attractive places of rest. Photovoltaic cells embedded in the roof, store energy to fuel the facilities in the common access zones.

Through a clever interplay of various constellations of spatial modules, the building is reminiscent of the legendary Rubik's Cube, a toy popular in the 1980s that challenged the coordination and intelligence of an entire generation.

Das Wohngebäude präsentiert sich in der dichten, heterogenen, von gründerzeitlicher Blockrandbebauung geprägten Umgebung als scharfkantiger monolithischer, matt schwarzer Kubus, den unregelmäßig gesetzte, hervortretende, helle Loggien kontrastreich aufladen. Diese raumhoch verglasten Loggien erweitern den Wohnraum in Richtung Park und sind gleichzeitig zentrales Fassadenelement im Wechselspiel mit dem filigranen Mosaik der frei gesetzten dunklen Eternit-Platten. Das weit auskragende, aus der Achse gedrehte und perforierte Flugdach relativiert die Strenge des Eckgebäudes und dynamisiert dessen oberen Abschluss. Die allgemein zugängliche Dachterrasse bietet mit einer Sauna und der dazugehörigen Ruhezone einen attraktiven Erholungsraum. In die Dachfläche eingelassene Photovoltaikzellen versorgen die gemeinschaftlichen Anlagen mit Energie.

In seinem raffinierten Spiel mit unterschiedlichen Konstellationen räumlicher Module erinnert das Haus an ein reales Spielzeug, nämlich an den legendären Rubik-Würfel, der in den 80er Jahren die Geschicklichkeit und Intelligenz einer ganzen Generation herausforderte.

STATE OF FLUX
Exhibition: Delugan Meissl Associated Architects
Location: kunst Meran / Merano arte
20.04.–09.07.2002
Exhibition area: 500 m^2
Photocredits: Delugan Meissl

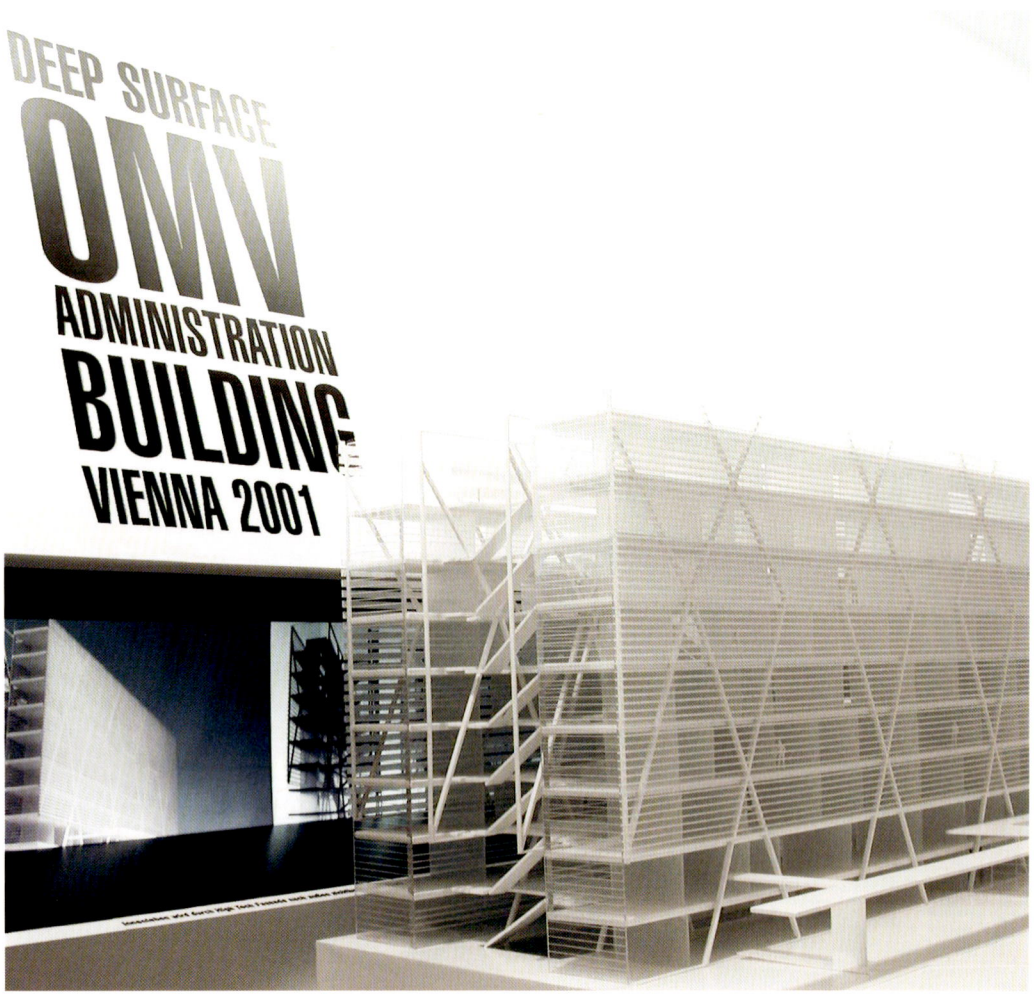

The exhibition in the Kunsthaus in Merano presented built and planned projects by the Vienna-based team and illustrated at the same time the manifold roles taken on by the younger generation of architects.

The five chapters did not only focus on Delugan Meissl Associated Architects' thematic priorities within their broad architectural spectrum, but also explained the concepts and design strategies behind them. The title "state of flux" is an approach to the design signature of the team, in which the sculptural and fluid elements are combined in a distinctive modern style.

In an architecture exhibition the exhibition design which lets the visitor directly experience the spatial ideas, is of special importance. A display system, especially designed for the space of the Kunsthaus, not only presented the exhibits, media and materials, but also reflected the "state of flux" in a visual, spatial way.

TOWNHOUSE WIMBERGERGASSE

RESIDENTIAL AND OFFICE BUILDING | VIENNA
Address: Wimbergergasse 14-16, 1070 Vienna
Client: Kallco Bauträger GmbH, Vienna
Construction period: 1999-2001
Site area: 2.900 m^2
Floor area: 5.700 m^2
Photocredits: M. Spiluttini, Delugan Meissl

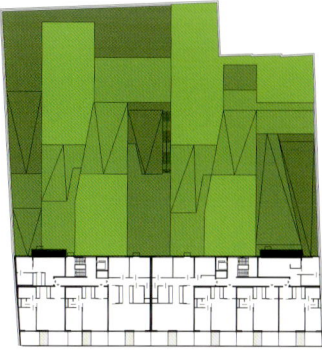

The Wimbergergasse Townhouse occupies a building gap that arose in the dense urban grid of Gründerzeit buildings. As a residential neighborhood, the district traditionally exhibits green courtyards with small commercial buildings. Despite its compactness as a part of a classical block development, the complex has an open, permeable character and is communicative, both in respect to the dialogue between the two wings, and the relation between old and new. The design displays two dominant design motifs – the accentuation of topography and the space-containing feature of the façade – that are merged fluidly both in a formal and functional sense. In the horizontal plane to the rear of the complex, office zones are arranged in layers on two to three flat levels. Vertically it is not the street-side façade of the residential wing that forms the outermost boundary, but instead a modular system of loggias and open spaces which extends beyond it and which is accentuated into a strong visual impulse. The apartments can be configured by sliding walls according to individual specifications, whereby a surprisingly rich array of possibilities both horizontally and vertically is offered.

Das Stadthaus besetzt eine Baulücke im dichten innerstädtischen Raster gründerzeitlicher Häuser. Die Umgebung bestimmen Wohnhäuser mit begrünten Höfen und niedrigen gewerblichen Bauten. Trotz der Kompaktheit als Teil einer klassischen Blockbebauung besitzt die Wohn- und Büroanlage einen offenen, durchlässigen Charakter und ermöglicht einen Dialog zwischen den beiden Trakten sowie zwischen Alt und Neu. Der Entwurf folgt zwei dominanten gestalterischen Leitmotiven, die sich formal und funktional schlüssig verbinden: der Akzentuierung der Topographie und der Raumhaltigkeit der Fassade. In der horizontalen Erstreckung des rückwärtigen Teils der Anlage werden die Bürozonen in zwei bis drei flachen Geschossen übereinander geschichtet. In vertikaler Richtung schließt die straßenseitige Fassade den Wohnungstrakt nicht wie üblich ab, sondern erweitert ihn über ein modulares System von Loggien und Lufträumen, die so zwischengeschaltet sind, dass sich ein spannendes Fassadenspiel ergibt. Die Wohnungen lassen sich durch verschiebbare Raumteiler individuell konfigurieren und überraschen durch eine Fülle an horizontalen und vertikalen Spielräumen.

Ce bâtiment urbain s'insère dans un territoire vacant au sein du réseau dense d'immeubles XIXe du centre-ville. L'environnement se compose d'immeubles aux cours végétalisées, où se dressent de petits bâtiments industriels. Malgré la compacité inhérente à toute construction classique en blocs, cet immeuble d'habitations et de bureaux au caractère ouvert et perméable établit un dialogue entre les deux ailes ainsi qu'entre l'ancien et le neuf. Le projet révèle deux principaux leitmotivs formels, l'accentuation de la topographie et la spatialité de la façade, qui s'unissent ici de façon résolument formelle et fonctionnelle : dans l'extension horizontale de la partie arrière, les zones de bureaux se superposent en deux à trois étages plats. Dans le sens vertical, la façade sur rue ne clôt pas l'ensemble d'appartements comme d'habitude, mais l'agrandit en un système modulaire de loggias et d'espaces aériens, qui se connectent les uns aux autres pour produire un jeu de façade captivant. Des séparations mobiles permettent de configurer à son goût les appartements, qui surprennent par l'abondance des possibilités horizontales comme verticales.

La casa ocupa un solar en la densa cuadrícula del centro urbano rodeado de edificios de la época Gründerzeit. El entorno viene determinado por casas de pisos con patios ajardinados, en los que se ubican pequeños negocios. A pesar de la estructura compacta que le es inherente como parte de un bloque clásico, el complejo de viviendas y oficinas posee un carácter abierto y permeable que permite el dialogo entre las dos alas, así como entre lo viejo y lo nuevo. El diseño muestra dos motivos creativos dominantes: la acentuación de la topografía y la especialidad de la fachada, que se unen aquí de modo concluyente en lo formal y lo funcional. En el plano horizontal y en la parte trasera del complejo, las zonas de oficina se superponen en dos e incluso tres plantas planas. En sentido vertical, la fachada de la calle no cierra el ala destinada a viviendas como suele ser lo normal, por el contrario, la amplía mediante un sistema modular de balcones y espacios abiertos intercalados de tal manera que dan lugar a una sugestiva imagen frontal. Las viviendas se pueden configurar de modo personal mediante paneles corredizos y sorprenden por el amplio margen de juego que crean tanto en sentido horizontal como vertical.

Questa casa di città occupa uno spazio libero nella fitta rete di palazzi della fine dell'Ottocento. L'ambiente circostante è caratterizzato da edifici residenziali con cortili verdi, nei quali si trovano basse costruzioni commerciali. Nonostante la compattezza tipica dei fabbricati a blocco, il complesso per appartamenti e uffici ha un carattere aperto e permette un dialogo tra le due sezioni e tra vecchio e nuovo. Il progetto mostra due motivi artistici di base dominanti – l'accentuazione della topografia e la spazialità della facciata – che si uniscono formalmente e funzionalmente in modo convincente: nell'estensione orizzontale della parte posteriore del complesso, gli uffici vengono stratificati uno sull'altro su due o tre piani. In direzione verticale, la facciata sul lato della strada non conclude come di consueto il tratto residenziale, ma lo amplia attraverso un sistema a moduli di logge e spazi aerei, che sono distribuiti in modo da creare un interessante gioco alterno. Gli appartamenti possono essere configurati individualmente grazie a elementi divisori scorrevoli e stupiscono per la ricchezza di spazi in direzione orizzontale e verticale.

MISCHEK TOWER
RESIDENTIAL BUILDING | DONAU-CITY VIENNA
Address: Leonard-Bernstein-Strasse 8, 1220 Vienna
Client: Mischek, Vienna
Construction period: 1996-2000
Site area: 6.296 m^2
Floor area: 44.393 m^2
Photocredits: M. Spiluttini

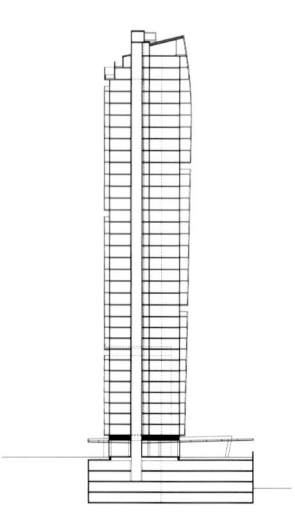

The Mischek Tower in the Donau-City was the office's first big commission. With its 35 storeys and a total height of 110 meters it is currently the tallest residential building in Austria. The tower is designed as a slab whose slender part is a reducing, upward tapering, slightly curving vertical that emerges out of a bar. It is a horizontal base construction that respects the height of its neighbouring buildings and establishes thus the dialogue with its environment as a high-rise complex.

The phenomenal view made it imperative to assign exterior space in form of loggias and terraces to each apartment. The parapets of the loggias are constructed half of aluminium and half of glass elements that has a fine litex-dot raster imprint. The architects developed a "façade interplay" with glass and aluminium elements that have been mounted facing each other so that no continuous rhythm is created optically. In all apartments can be individually added glass folding elements which, even if installed in an irregular pattern, will not harm the already playful rhythmic façade but contribute to the overall liveliness.

Because of the building's shape and the façade's composition, the Mischek Tower – despite its enormous dimensions – appears almost light. Its mass nearly dissolves in the transparency and the reflections of the glass-aluminium elements.

Der Mischek Tower in der Wiener Donau-City stellt den ersten großen Auftrag für Delugan Meissl Associated Architects dar. Mit 35 Stockwerken auf 110 Metern Gesamthöhe ist der Turm das derzeit höchste Wohnhaus Österreichs. Das Gebäude präsentiert sich als Scheibe, deren schmale Seite als nach oben verjüngende, leicht gekrümmte Vertikale aus einem Riegel emporwächst, welcher als horizontaler Sockelbau die Höhe der umliegenden Bebauung aufnimmt und den Dialog des Hochhauskomplexes mit der Umgebung herstellt.

Die phänomenale Fernsicht erforderte es geradezu, jeder Wohnung Freiräume in Form von Loggien und Terrassen zuzuordnen. Die Brüstungen der Loggien sind teils aus Aluminium, teils aus Glas, das mit einem filigranen weißen Punktraster bedruckt wurde, gefertigt. Die Architekten entwickelten aus diesen zwei Materialien ein Fassadenspiel gegeneinander versetzter, sich wiederholender, aber zufällig erscheinender Elemente. Die Bewohner haben die Möglichkeit, rahmenlose auffaltbare Verglasungen individuell hinzuzufügen. Auch wenn diese unregelmäßig zum Einsatz kommen, gefährden sie das ohnehin sehr spielerisch rhythmisierte Fassadenbild nicht, sondern beleben es ganz im Gegenteil weiter.

Durch die Baukörperausbildung und die Fassadengestaltung wirkt der Mischek Tower trotz seiner gewaltigen Dimension geradezu leicht, seine Masse löst sich in der Transparenz und Reflexion der Glas- und Aluminiumelemente nahezu auf.

La Mischek Tower de Donau-City, à Vienne, représente la première grosse commande du studio viennois. Cet édifice de 35 étages sur une hauteur totale de 110 mètres est actuellement la plus haute tour d'habitation en Autriche. Il se présente comme un disque, dont le côté étroit est une verticale légèrement courbée et s'amenuisant vers le haut, qui se dresse sur une barre. Ce socle horizontal s'aligne sur la hauteur des constructions adjacentes et instaure un dialogue entre la tour et son environnement.

La vue fabuleuse imposait en quelque sorte de faire bénéficier chaque appartement d'espaces libres sous forme de loggias et de terrasses. Les parapets des loggias sont fabriqués pour partie en aluminium, pour partie en verre imprimé d'un réseau de points blancs en filigrane. À partir de ces deux matériaux, les architectes ont élaboré un jeu de façade, où s'opposent et se répètent des éléments qui néanmoins semblent aléatoires. Les habitants ont la possibilité d'ajouter à titre individuel des vitrages sans cadre et pliables. Si ceux-ci sont utilisés de manière irrégulière, ils ne nuisent en rien à l'aspect ludique et rythmé de la façade, mais au contraire, l'animent encore davantage.

La Mischek Tower, par la constitution de ses différents corps et de sa façade, paraît vraiment surprenant légère en dépit de ses dimensions imposantes, sa masse semble se dissoudre dans la transparence et les reflets des éléments en verre et en aluminium.

La Mischek Tower, situada en el nuevo barrio vienés Donau-City, constituyó el primer gran encargo para el despacho de Viena. Con 35 pisos y una altura total de 110 metros, la torre es actualmente el edificio de viviendas más alto de Austria. Tiene el aspecto de un prisma rectangular cuya cara más estrecha, ligeramente curvada y estrechándose en punta, se eleva en vertical sobre un bloque, que a modo de base horizontal, toma la altura de los edificios circundantes y crea un diálogo entre el rascacielos y su entorno.

La fenomenal panorámica prácticamente exigía que cada vivienda dispusiera de espacios libres en forma de balcones y terrazas. Las balaustradas de los balcones son en parte de aluminio y en parte de cristal grabado con un punteado blanco en filigrana. A partir de esos dos materiales los arquitectos desarrollaron en la fachada un juego de elementos que se superponen y repiten, pero cuya aparición no deja de ser casual. A los habitantes del edificio se les dio la posibilidad de añadir voluntariamente cristaleras plegables y sin marco. La irregular aplicación de estos elementos no hace peligrar el ritmo juguetón de la fachada por el contrario, más bien lo revitaliza.

El desarrollo de su estructura y la configuración de la fachada consiguen que la Mischek Tower parezca ligera a pesar de su considerable tamaño. Su volumen se disuelve en la transparencia y los reflejos de los elementos de aluminio y cristal.

La Mischek Tower nella Donau-City di Vienna rappresenta il primo grande incarico per Delugan Meissl Associated Architects. In questo momento la torre con i suoi 35 piani e 110 metri d'altezza è il complesso abitativo più alto dell'Austria. L'edificio si presenta come un disco, la cui parte più stretta si rastrema verso l'alto come una verticale leggermente curvata, con la base su una traversa. Quest'ultima, una sorta di zoccolo orizzontale, riprende l'altezza delle costruzioni circostanti e apre il dialogo del grattacielo con i dintorni.

Il panorama fenomenale ha reso assolutamente necessaria l'attribuzione a ogni appartamento di spazi liberi sotto forma di logge e terrazze. Le balaustre delle terrazze sono in parte in alluminio, in parte in vetro su cui è stato stampato un fine reticolo di punti bianchi. Con questi due materiali gli architetti hanno creato sulla facciata un gioco di elementi spostati uno rispetto all'altro, che si ripetono, ma che sembrano casuali. Gli inquilini hanno la possibilità di aggiungere individualmente vetrate pieghevoli senza cornice. Anche se queste sono impiegate in modo irregolare, non compromettono l'aspetto comunque ritmico e giocoso della facciata, anzi lo ravvivano ulteriormente.

Per via della forma del fabbricato e dell'impostazione della facciata la Mischek Tower sembra addirittura leggera, nonostante le dimensioni enormi; la sua massa, infatti, scompare quasi nella trasparenza e nel riflesso degli elementi in vetro e alluminio.

HAUS J, ABSAM
SINGLE FAMILY HOUSE / EXTENSION | TYROL
Client: Private
Construction period: 1998-2000
Site area: 409 m^2
Floor area: 281 m^2
Photocredits: M. Spiluttini, Delugan Meissl

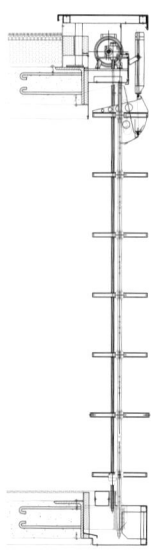

In the tyrolean place of pilgrimage a living unit for a small family, directly inserted alongside the church, had to complete an existing saddle roof house. It rests on the base of an old structure. Inside the transparent living box floor differences and level leaps are interwoven and result in a highly spatial complexity.

A façade structured by glass louvers characterizes the living floor. The viennese office developed especially for House J a system of glass slats including a liquid crystal layer. The glass curtains can be opened and closed by section, and electronic impulses sent to the liquid crystal layer of the plates turn them from completely transparent to milky opaque. Behind the high-tech façade a 1,80-meter wide loggia zone encircles the house and can be separated from or incorporated into the house's interior via a second glass skin with sliding doors at given points. Thanks to the multi-functional façade that gives an impression of space, it is largely up to the inhabitants to determine the boundaries of House J and to use the intermediate zone in a flexible way.

With House J the architects transform their visions of flowing spatial sequences within a strict orthogonal grid. Not the form itself becomes fluid but the dynamic ductus arises through the multilateral form of the transitions – whether it be through the variable permeability of the glass façade or through the way the individual volumes have been interwoven.

In dem Tiroler Wallfahrtsort wurde unmittelbar neben der Kirche als Ergänzung zu einem bestehenden Satteldachhaus eine neue Wohneinheit für eine Kleinfamilie errichtet. Den Sockel für den Neubau bilden Teile eines älteren Gebäudes. Im Inneren der transparenten Wohnbox bietet ein Geflecht aus Höhendifferenzen und Niveausprüngen höchste räumliche Komplexität.

Das Wohngeschoss kennzeichnet eine an drei Seiten umlaufende, durch horizontale Glaslamellen strukturierte Fassade. Das Wiener Büro entwickelte eigens für Haus J ein gläsernes Lamellensystem mit einer eingeschlossenen Flüssigkristallschicht. Die LCD-Glas-Schwerter können per Fernsteuerung geöffnet, geschlossen und auch undurchsichtig gemacht werden. Hinter der Hightech Fassade läuft eine 1,80 Meter tiefe Loggia, die sich über eine zweite, an einigen Stellen verschiebbare Glashaut vom Innenraum abgrenzt beziehungsweise mit ihm verbindet. Dank der raumbildenden, multifunktionalen Fassade können die Bewohner die Grenzen des Hauses weitgehend selbst bestimmen und die dabei entstehenden Zwischenbereiche flexibel nutzen.

Mit Haus J realisieren die Architekten ihre Vorstellungen von fließenden räumlichen Zusammenhängen im Rahmen eines orthogonalen Rasters. Nicht die Form selbst gerät dabei in Fluss, sondern die Dynamik entsteht durch die differenzierten Übergänge – sei es durch die variable Durchlässigkeit der Glasfassade oder durch die Verschachtelung der einzelnen Volumina.

Une nouvelle unité d'habitation pour une petite famille est venue s'adjoindre à une maison au toit en bâtière, jouxtant l'église de ce petit village du pèlerinage tyrolien. Certaines parties d'un bâtiment ancien ont été conservées pour lui tenir lieu de socle. Un tissu de hauteurs et de niveaux différents crée une extrême complexité spatiale à l'intérieur de la boîte habitable transparente.

Sur trois côtés, les façades structurées par des jalousies horizontales en verre caractérisent l'étage d'habitation. L'agence de Vienne a développé, spécialement pour la Maison J, un système de jalousies dont le verre renferme une couche de cristaux liquides. Ces glaives LCD s'ouvrent, se ferment ou s'opacifient par télécommande. Derrière la façade high tech court une loggia d'une profondeur de 1,80 mètre, qu'une deuxième peau en verre, coulissante à certains endroits, sépare ou relie avec l'espace intérieur. Grâce à cette façade multifonctions, les habitants peuvent déterminer eux-mêmes, dans une large mesure, les limites de la maison, et utiliser avec souplesse les zones intermédiaires ainsi créées.

Par la Maison J, les architectes concrétisent leurs notions de fluidité des rapports spatiaux dans le cadre d'une trame orthogonale. Ici, ce n'est pas la forme elle-même qui devient fluide, mais la dynamique qui découle des transitions différenciées – que ce soit par la transparence variable de la façade en verre ou par l'imbrication des différents volumes.

En el lugar de peregrinación tirolés se construyó una nueva vivienda para una pequeña familia como anexo a una casa con tejado de dos vertientes, que existía ya en la inmediata vecindad de la iglesia. Partes del antiguo edificio se conservaron como base para la nueva construcción. En el interior de la caja transparente, un entramado de diferentes alturas y cambios de nivel ofrece la mayor complejidad espacial.

La vivienda se caracteriza por la fachada continua que recorre tres de sus lados estructurada a base de láminas de cristal horizontales. Para la casa J, el despacho vienés desarrolló su propio sistema de láminas de cristal con una capa integrada de cristal líquido. Por mando a distancia se puede abrir y cerrar las placas de cristal-LCD y también volverlas completamente opacas. Tras de la fachada de alta tecnología transcurre una galería de 1,80 metros de profundidad que se separa o une al espacio interior mediante una segunda capa de cristal que en algunos puntos es corrediza. Gracias a las fachadas multifuncionales y distribuidoras del espacio, los habitantes pueden determinar por sí mismos continuamente los límites de la casa y aprovechar de un modo flexible las zonas intermedias que así se crean.

Con la casa J los arquitectos hacen realidad sus ideas de conexión espacial continua en el marco de una cuadrícula ortogonal. La forma en sí no es la que se convierte en fluido, es más bien la dinámica, la que se crea por medio de las transiciones diferenciadas, ya sea mediante la transparencia variable de la fachada de cristal o mediante la maraña de los volúmenes individuales.

Nel luogo di pellegrinaggio tirolese, direttamente accanto alla chiesa, è stata costruita una nuova unità abitativa per una piccola famiglia, a complemento dell'esistente edificio col tetto a due falde. Come base del nuovo fabbricato sono state mantenute parti di una costruzione preesistente. All'interno del trasparente box abitabile, l'intreccio di differenze d'altezza e salti di livello crea un'alta complessità di spazi.

Il piano giorno è caratterizzato su tre lati da una facciata strutturata a lamelle in vetro. Lo studio viennese ha creato apposta per House J un sistema di lamelle di vetro con uno strato interno di cristalli liquidi. Per mezzo di un telecomando le spade di vetro e cristalli possono essere aperte, chiuse e anche rese opache. Dietro la facciata high-tech corre una loggia profonda 1,80 metri, separata dallo spazio abitativo da un'ulteriore vetrata, scorrevole in alcuni punti. Grazie alla facciata multifunzionale creatrice di spazi, gli inquilini stessi sono in grado di definire i confini della casa e di usarne gli spazi intermedi a seconda delle esigenze.

Con House J gli architetti realizzano la loro concezione di relazioni spaziali fluide in una struttura ortogonale. In questo modo, non è la forma che diventa fluida, al contrario, la dinamicità risulta dai passaggi differenziati: sia attraverso la trasparenza variabile della facciata in vetro, sia per mezzo del concatenamento dei singoli volumi.

OBERLAA HOUSING DEVELOPMENT
SOCIAL HOUSING | VIENNA
Address: Areal Grundäcker, 1010 Vienna
Client: Mischek, Vienna
Construction period: 1997-1998
Site Area: 9.667 m²
Floor Area: 9.495 m²
Photocredits: G. Erlacher, Delugan Meissl

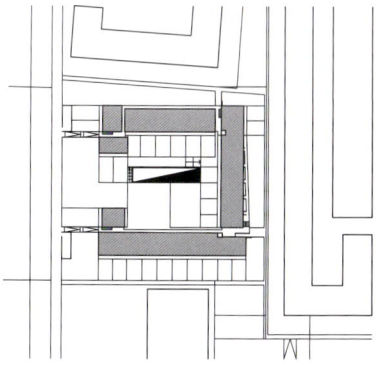

This social housing project on the periphery is the first of the so-called "developer competition" in Vienna and is to be one of the cheapest recent residential building projects. The city's parameters were set out with very high ecological aims while the economic input was to be kept at a minimum. One therefore had to plan as simply and economically as possible while providing the inhabitants with a high quality of life.

The apartments are accessible via covered aisles and are largely "false maisonettes" which means they can be reached via internal staircases. They offer extensive space and necessary storage room.

The classical perimeter block development was dropped in favour of an open courtyard structure with surrounding row and solitary structures. This results not only in optimal light conditions for the apartments but also in the best possible pedestrian guidance system throughout the building complex.

In order to keep costs to a minimum, industrially prefabricated elements are employed for identical modules. Apart from using such large scale and prefabricated concrete skeleton elements, the façade is made out of multi-layer boards reinforced with aluminium which front the loggia layer and act as a semi-transparent filter. This punched membrane, together with the moveable sun elements, lends the building its import and its playful casual appearance.

Bei dem sozialen Wohnbau an der städtischen Peripherie handelt es sich um den ersten so genannten „Bauträger-Wettbewerb" in Wien und einen der kostengünstigsten Wohnbauten der letzten Jahre. Das städtebauliche Leitkonzept war vorgegeben, das ökologische Ziel hochgesteckt und das ökonomische Limit extrem niedrig. Es galt also, so einfach und kostensparend wie möglich zu planen und dabei den Bewohnern trotzdem eine hohe Wohnqualität zu garantieren.

Die Wohnungen werden über Laubengänge erschlossen und sind größtenteils als „falsche Maisonetten" ausgebildet, werden also über eine interne Treppe erreicht und bieten so großzügigen Luftraum und notwendige Stauflächen.

Die klassische Blockrandbebauung wurde zugunsten einer offenen Hofstruktur aufgegeben und in Zeilen- und Solitärbauten aufgelöst. Daraus resultiert nicht nur eine optimale Belichtung der Wohnungen, sondern auch eine bestmögliche Wegeführung innerhalb der Anlage.

Um besonders wirtschaftlich zu bauen, setzte man auf industrielle Vorfertigung und die Addition gleicher Module. Neben der Verwendung von Großtafelelementen und Betonskelett-Fertigteilen kam eine Fassadenverkleidung aus aluminiumverstärkten Mehrschichtplatten zum Einsatz, die der Loggienschicht als semitransparenter Filter vorgelagert wurde. Diese gelochte Membran verleiht dem Wohnbau in Verbindung mit verschiebbaren Sonnenelementen seine Signifikanz und ein spielerisches, weil zufälliges Erscheinungsbild.

Cet immeuble de logements sociaux situé à la périphérie résulte du premier « concours pour promoteur-constructeur » à Vienne et est l'un des chantiers les moins onéreux de ces dernières années. Le principe directeur urbanistique était donné, l'objectif écologique élevé et la marge financière extrêmement réduite. L'enjeu consistait donc à mettre au point un projet aussi simple et peu coûteux que possible, tout en offrant aux habitants une qualité de vie élevée.

Les appartements, auxquels on accède par des arcades, sont en grande partie des duplex possédant de ce fait un escalier intérieur, d'où un grand espace d'air et des rangements indispensables.

À la construction classique en blocs, les architectes ont préféré une cour ouverte ainsi qu'une disposition en rangées parallèles ou en édifices isolés. Ainsi, non seulement les appartements bénéficient d'un éclairage maximal, mais le cheminement à l'intérieur de l'ensemble est optimisé.

Pour construire à un niveau de prix particulièrement bas, la préfabrication industrielle et la modularisation s'imposaient. De grands panneaux ont été employés, ainsi que des éléments préfabriqués pour le squelette en béton, parallèlement à un revêtement de façade en plaques multicouches renforcées en aluminium, que l'on a posées devant la couche des loggias à la façon d'un filtre transparent. Cette membrane percée, avec les panneaux solaires mobiles, confère à l'immeuble sa signification et un aspect ludique puisque aléatoire.

Las viviendas sociales en la periferia constituyeron el primero de los llamados "concursos de promotores" de Viena y fueron unas de las viviendas más asequibles de los últimos años. La directriz urbanística estaba determinada, el listón ecológico se encontraba muy alto y el presupuesto era extremadamente bajo. Se trataba pues de planificar del modo más sencillo y económico posible proporcionando además a los inquilinos una elevada calidad de vida.

Los apartamentos a los que se accede por medio de galerías abiertas, están construidos en gran parte como "falsos dúplex", es decir con acceso por medio de una escalera interna, y ofrecen mucho espacio abierto así como las necesarias superficies de almacenaje.

La clásica disposición en manzana rectangular se descartó en pro de una estructura de patio abierta y se resolvió mediante edificios aislados y en línea. Como resultado no sólo se logró la iluminación óptima de los pisos, sino también el mejor transcurso itinerario en el interior del complejo.

Para construir económicamente se recurrió al prefabricado industrial y a la adición de módulos iguales. Además de emplear grandes paneles y piezas prefabricadas del armazón de cemento, se utilizó un revestimiento de fachada a base de planchas de varias capas reforzadas de aluminio, que se colocaron como filtro ante la capa de las galerías. Esta membrana perforada, junto con elementos móviles para proteger del sol proporciona al edificio significación y una imagen caprichosa debido a su carácter casual.

L'edilizia residenziale convenzionata nella periferia è stata eretta nel primo concorso di costruttori a Vienna e costituisce uno dei fabbricati meno costosi degli ultimi anni. Il concetto urbanistico di base era predeterminato, la mira ecologica alta e il margine economico estremamente basso. Si trattava quindi di fare un progetto il più semplice e conveniente possibile, ma, ciononostante, di garantire agli inquilini un'alta qualità di abitabilità.

Gli appartamenti sono accessibili attraverso ballatoi e sono costruiti come false maisonette, si raggiungono quindi attraverso una scala interna e offrono così molto spazio e le necessarie superfici di rimessa.

Al classico palazzo a blocco è stata preferita una struttura a corte aperta, divisa in singoli fabbricati a riga. Così ne risultano non solo un'esposizione ideale degli appartamenti, ma anche tragitti più favorevoli all'interno del complesso.

Per costruire in modo particolarmente conveniente si è puntato su prefabbricati industriali e sulla sovrapposizione di moduli uguali. Oltre all'uso di grandi lastre e di elementi prefabbricati di calcestruzzo per la struttura, è stato impiegato per la facciata un rivestimento in lastre a vari strati, rinforzate di alluminio; a questo è stato poi anteposto il piano delle logge come un filtro trasparente. Questa membrana forata combinata con elementi solari scorrevoli conferisce all'edificio una certa importanza e un aspetto giocoso, poiché casuale.

BEAM

RESIDENTIAL BUILDING WITH OFFICES
AND A KINDERGARTEN | DONAU-CITY VIENNA

Address: Leonard-Bernstein-Straße 4-6, 1220 Vienna
Client: Donaucity Wohnbau AG, Vienna
Construction period: 1996-1998
Site area: 5.592 m^2
Floor area: 20.442 m^2
Photocredits: M. Spiluttini, Liedl & Gronemann

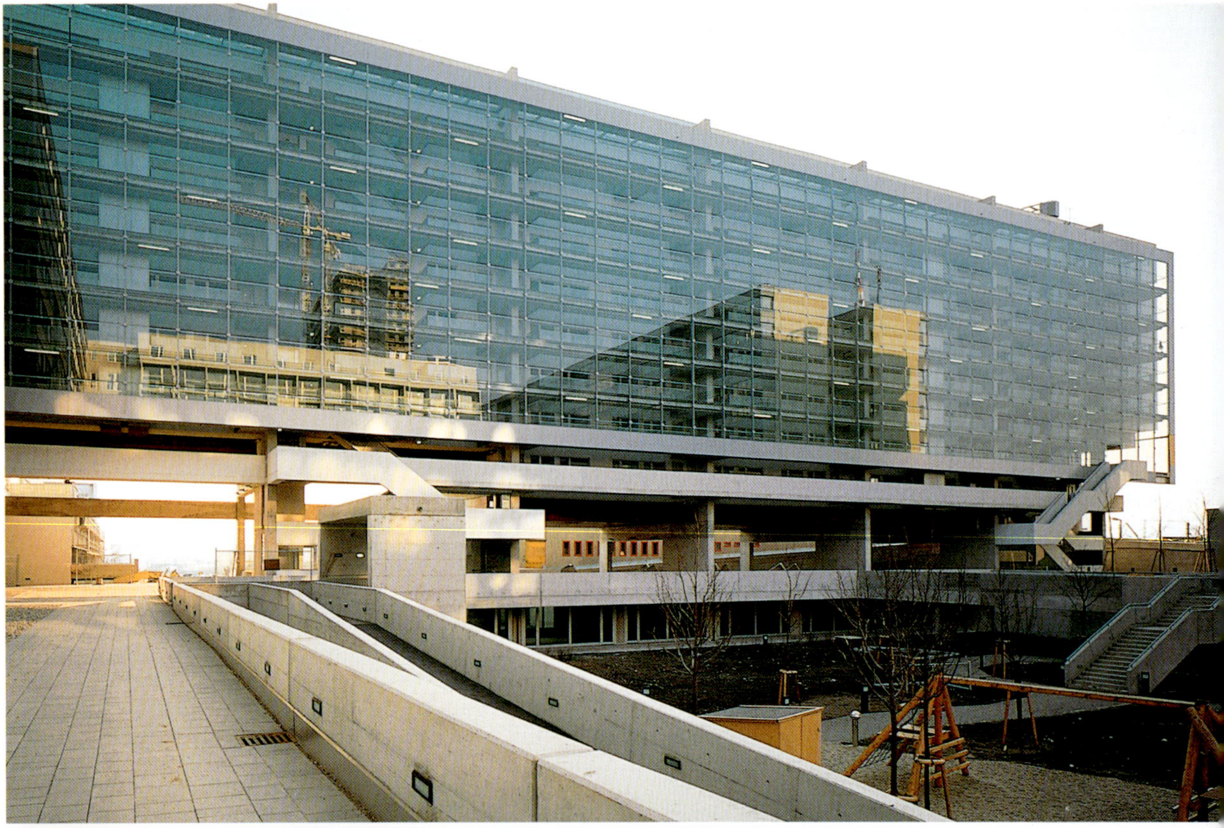

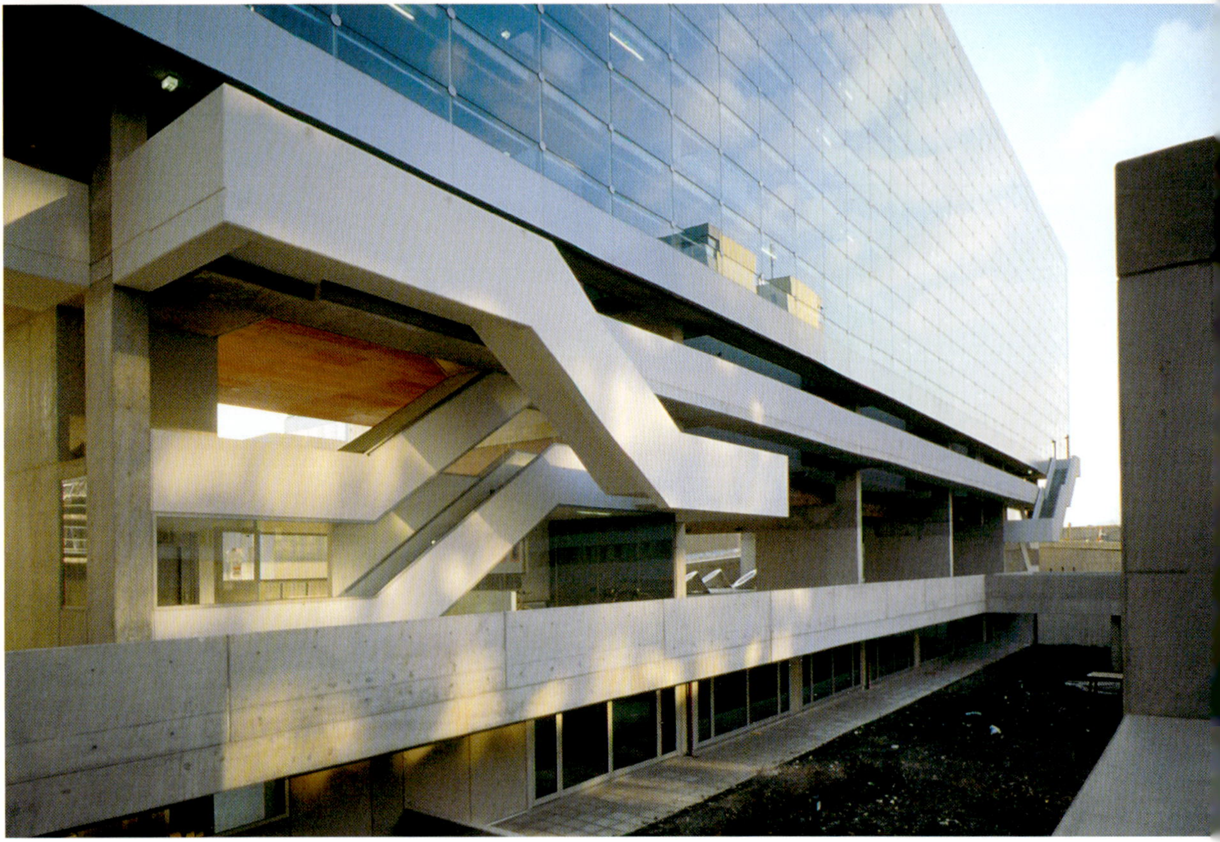

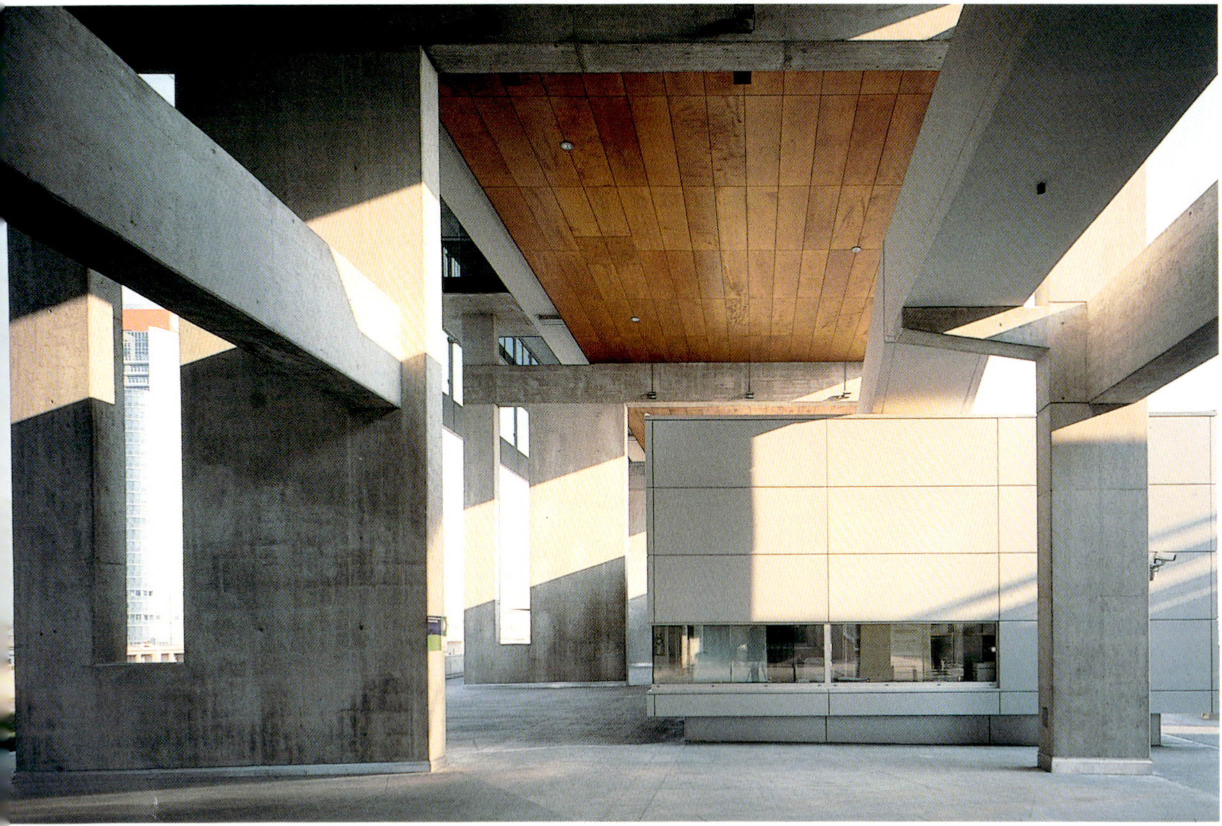

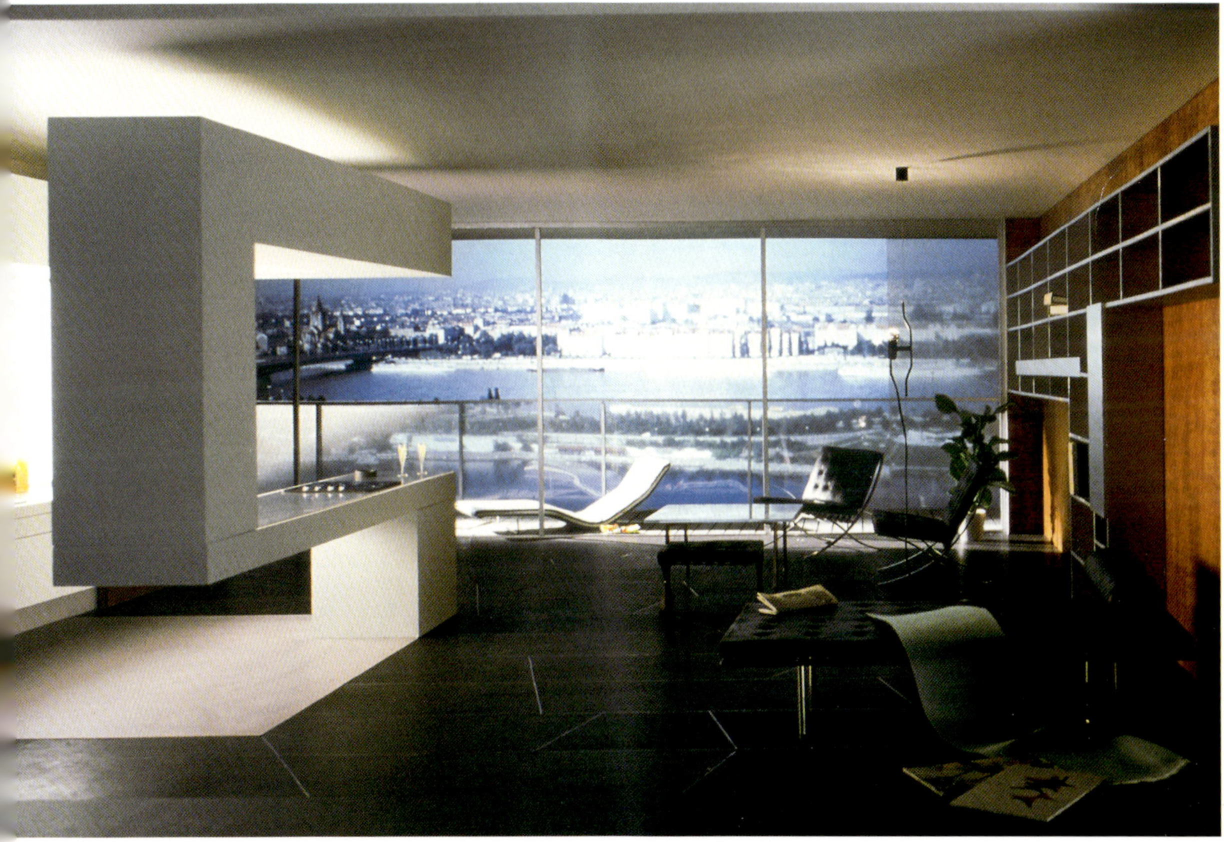

The concise form of the "horizontal high-rise" and the highly visible location of this apartment complex referred to as the "Beam" signal, at first glance, its individualistic conception. This recumbent apartment building follows the shoreline of the New Danube along its entire 180-meters length. The seven-story, enormous but transparent building is supported by pilotis which vary in height between ten and four meters and thus create spaces of different size. This opening affords not only a spatial visibility for the buildings behind it, but also ensures that this apartment complex is regularly washed by the overlap and fringe of the public sphere. With its riverside apartments, the "Beam" offers inhabitants a truly spectacular view of the river and the historic center of Vienna. The 190 apartments extend from front to back, some of them are maisonnettes and have both glazed loggias and glass vestibules that form a part of the network of walkways for entering the apartments along the glazed backs of the building. In keeping with the given urban planning situation but also with contemporary living habits, this building is not a mere "living apparatus" but rather an open "container" for urban living that offers ample space for diverse lifestyles and succeeds in a distinct urban quality.

Die prägnante Form des „horizontalen Hochhauses" und die exponierte Lage des als „Balken" bezeichneten Wohnbaus signalisieren schon auf den ersten Blick seine individuelle Konzeption. Über eine Gesamtlänge von 180 Metern folgt der liegende Wohnblock dem Uferverlauf der Neuen Donau. Der siebengeschossige mächtige, aber transparent ausgebildete Baukörper ist aufgeständert. Die Stützenhöhe variiert zwischen zehn und vier Metern, wodurch unterschiedliche Freiräume entstehen. Dieser offene Sockelbereich fungiert einerseits als Sehspalt für die dahinter liegenden Wohnbauten und sorgt andererseits dafür, dass Aktivitäten des öffentlichen Raums den Wohnbau unterspülen. Die Bewohner genießen von diesem privilegierten Standort aus eine spektakuläre Aussicht auf den Fluss und die Altstadt Wiens. Die 190 durchgesteckten Wohnungen sind teilweise als Maisonetten ausgebildet und besitzen eine verglaste Loggia sowie einen gläsernen Vorraum als Teil des Geflechts von Laubengängen, über die die Wohnungen von der ebenfalls verglasten Rückseite erschlossen werden. Der städtebaulichen Situation, aber auch den heutigen Lebensgewohnheiten entsprechend, wurde hier keine reine „Wohnmaschine", sondern ein bewohnbarer offener „Behälter" positioniert, der unterschiedlichen Lebensstilen Platz bietet und eine deutlich urbane Wohnqualität erreicht.

La forme dense de la « tour horizontale » et la situation exposée de cet immeuble d'habitation qualifié de « poutre » signalent sa conception individuelle dès le premier regard. Le bloc couché suit le contour des rives du Nouveau Danube sur une longueur totale de 180 mètres. Cette construction de sept étages, imposante mais transparente, est montée sur des supports hauts de dix, sept et quatre mètres, d'où des espacements variés. D'une part ce socle ouvert laisse passer le regard pour les constructions situées derrière, d'autre part, il assure le flux et le reflux des activités de l'espace public. Depuis ce point de vue privilégié, les habitants jouissent d'une vue spectaculaire sur le fleuve et la vieille ville. Conçus en partie comme des duplex, les 190 appartements sont ouverts de part en part par une loggia et un hall vitré, lequel s'inscrit dans le réseau d'arcades permettant d'accéder aux appartements depuis la façade arrière, également en verre. Conformément à la situation urbanistique, mais aussi aux modes de vie actuels, ce n'est pas une « machine à habiter » qui prend place ici, mais un « conteneur » habitable et ouvert, qui accueille divers styles de vie et offre une qualité d'habitat d'un grand raffinement.

La expresiva forma del "rascacielos horizontal" y el visible emplazamiento del edificio de viviendas conocido como "travesaño" demuestran ya a primera vista su concepción individual. Sobre una longitud total de 180 metros el edificio yaciente se prolonga a lo largo de la orilla del Nuevo Danúbio. La estructura de siete pisos, imponente pero transparente, se apoya en pilares cuya altura varía entre diez y cuatro metros, de manera que se crean espacios libres de diferente dimensión. Esta zona de base abierta sirve por una parte como hendidura visual para los edificios situados detrás y por otra, se encarga de que las actividades del espacio público socaven el espacio residencial. Desde este emplazamiento privilegiado sus habitantes disfrutan de una espectacular panorámica del río y del casco antiguo de Viena. A lo largo del edificio se extienden 190 viviendas, algunas de ellas construidas como dúplex. Todas disponen de un balcón acristalado y de un vestíbulo de cristal como parte del entramado de galerías que dan acceso a los pisos de la parte trasera igualmente acristalada. De acuerdo con la situación urbanística, pero también con los hábitos de vida contemporáneos, no se ubicó aquí una mera máquina para vivir sino un "receptáculo" abierto y habitable que ofrece lugar para diferentes formas de vida y consigue una indudable calidad de vida urbana.

La forma pregnante del "grattacielo orizzontale" e la posizione esposta dell'edificio detto "trave" fanno notare sin dal primo sguardo la sua particolarità. L'edificio disteso segue l'andamento della riva del Nuovo Danubio per una lunghezza complessiva di 180 metri. L'imponente ma trasparente fabbricato a sette piani è rialzato su pilastri: l'altezza delle colonne varia tra 10 e 4 metri, creando in questo modo spazi liberi di diverse dimensioni. Questa base aperta funge da un lato come spiraglio per gli edifici situati nella parte posteriore, dall'altro consente che le attività proprie dello spazio pubblico si svolgano sotto l'edificio. Da questo luogo privilegiato gli inquilini godono di un panorama spettacolare sul fiume e sul centro storico di Vienna. Alcuni dei 190 appartamenti sono a due piani e dispongono di una loggia e di un atrio, ambedue a vetri, integrati in un intreccio di ballatoi, attraverso cui si accede agli appartamenti dal retro. Partendo dalla considerazione della situazione urbanistica, ma anche delle abitudini di vita attuali, in questo luogo non si è collocato un "edificio-macchina", ma un "recipiente" aperto e abitabile, che dà spazio ai più diversi stili di vita e raggiunge un livello decisamente urbano di abitabilità.

APARTMENTS STEIGENTESCHGASSE
RESIDENTIAL BUILDING | VIENNA
Address: Steigenteschgasse 26, 1220 Vienna
Client: Neues Leben, Vienna
Construction period: 2005-2006
Site area: 883 m^2
Floor area: 643 m^2

This concept for an apartment building on the outskirts of Vienna – to be built in an existing gap between buildings – will have the ground floor level slightly set back from the street while the upper levels form a continuous front with the other buildings. As a result the roofed entrance area will be protected. The foyer opens up its urban surroundings and continues them in the form of topographical elements and ramps while at the same time enabling diagonal access to the courtyard and garden. The typology of the ground plan of the four-in-hand building results from the attractiveness of the north-south alignment of the quoins, each of which house two flats. Open loggias as well as the generously laid out ground plan characterise the building. In order to increase the unit's plasticity the gutter line is partially raised by means of bays and alvoces. A fractal pattern of irregular window openings on both the southern and the northern façades creates differing valencies of the interior atmosphere and invokes different lines of vision as well as acting as a filter between interior and exterior. The façade thus becomes an identity forming graphical element and is a purely functional result from the very specific relationship between the apartments to their environment.

Die Erdgeschosszone des für eine Baulücke am Wiener Stadtrand konzipierten Mehrfamilienhauses ist von der Baulinie zurückgesetzt, während die oberen Geschosse die an der Straße liegende Baugrenze aufgreifen. Auf diese Weise wird die Eingangssituation als geschützter überdachter Bereich ausgebildet. Das Foyer öffnet sich dem städtischen Umfeld, greift dieses in Form topographischer Elemente und Rampen auf und ermöglicht gleichzeitig eine diagonale Durchquerung zum Hof und Garten. Die Grundrisstypologie des Vierspänners resultiert aus der Attraktivität der nach Norden und Süden ausgerichteten Schmalseiten, die jeweils zwei Wohnungen beinhalten. Offene Loggien sind neben den großzügig geschnittenen Grundrissen gebäudecharakteristisch. Um die Plastizität des Baukörpers zu steigern, wird die Traufenkante partiell mit Erkern oder Gaupen überhöht. An der Nord- und Südfassade erzielt ein fraktales Muster von unregelmäßig geformten Fensteröffnungen unterschiedliche Wertigkeiten der inneren Raumstimmungen. Es evoziert verschiedene Blickrichtungen und ist zugleich differenzierter Filter zwischen Innen und Außen. Die Fassade wird zum identitätsbildenden, grafischen Element und resultiert ganz funktional aus dem spezifischen Außenraumbezug der Wohnungen.

Le rez-de-chaussée de cette maison, destinée à un territoire vacant situé aux confins de la capitale autrichienne, est en retrait par rapport à l'alignement, contrairement aux étages supérieurs. Ainsi, la situation de l'entrée se conçoit comme une zone protégée et couverte. Le hall d'entrée s'ouvre sur l'environnement citadin et s'en saisit sous forme d'éléments topographiques et de rampes. Parallèlement, il permet la traversée en diagonale vers la cour et le jardin. La typologie de ce quadrige résulte de l'attractivité des petits côtés orientés au nord et au sud, qui contiennent chacun deux appartements. L'édifice se caractérise par ses loggias ouvertes, ainsi que par les plans au sol généreux. Pour rehausser la plasticité de l'édifice, l'arête des chéneaux est en partie relevée par des encorbellements ou des lucarnes. Sur les façades nord et sud, un motif fractal d'ouvertures irrégulières transpose les ambiances des pièces à l'intérieur. Il évoque plusieurs perspectives, tout en tenant lieu de filtre différencié entre intérieur et extérieur. La façade devient un élément graphique générateur d'identité et résulte de façon très fonctionnelle du rapport spécifique à l'extérieur qu'entretiennent les appartements.

Para un espacio vacío entre dos edificios situado a las afueras de Viena se concibió una casa de pisos, cuya planta baja se retira de la línea de edificación, mientras que los pisos superiores llegan hasta el límite. De este modo la entrada se convierte en una zona protegida bajo techo. El vestíbulo se abre al entorno urbano y lo hace suyo mediante elementos topográficos y rampas. A la vez permite atravesar en diagonal hacia el patio y el jardín. La tipología de planta rectangular resulta del atractivo de los dos lados estrechos orientados al norte y al sur, cada uno de los cuales contiene dos pisos. El edificio se caracteriza por los balcones y la generosa distribución de las plantas. Para incrementar la plasticidad del edificio, el alero se eleva parcialmente con tragaluces y saledizos. Tanto en la fachada norte como en la sur, un diseño fractal conseguido a base de aberturas para las ventanas practicadas irregularmente consigue diferentes valencias de los efectos espaciales internos. Evoca perspectivas distintas y actúa a la vez como filtro entre el interior y el exterior. La fachada se convierte en elemento gráfico de identidad y es el resultado totalmente funcional de la relación específica con el espacio exterior de las viviendas.

Nella casa plurifamiliare, concepita per colmare un vuoto nella periferia di Vienna, il piano terra è arretrato rispetto al confine del sito, mentre i piani superiori ne riprendono la linea sulla strada. In questo modo l'ingresso rimane protetto e coperto. Il foyer si apre all'ambiente urbano circostante e lo richiama con elementi topografici e rampe. Allo stesso tempo permette di raggiungere cortile e giardino attraverso un percorso diagonale. La tipologia della pianta a tiro a quattro deriva dalla posizione ideale dei lati minori rivolti a nord e a sud che comprendono due appartamenti l'uno. Oltre agli spazi dal taglio generoso, un'altra caratteristica della costruzione sono le logge aperte. Per aumentare la plasticità della costruzione, la linea della grondaia è parzialmente rialzata con bovindi o abbaini. Sulle facciate a nord e a sud un motivo frattale di finestre a forma irregolare conferisce diverse valenze all'atmosfera degli ambienti interni. Esso evoca anche varie direzioni di sguardi e allo stesso tempo funge come filtro differenziato tra interno e esterno. La facciata diventa un elemento grafico di creazione d'identità e risulta in modo funzionale dallo specifico rapporto degli appartamenti con l'esterno.

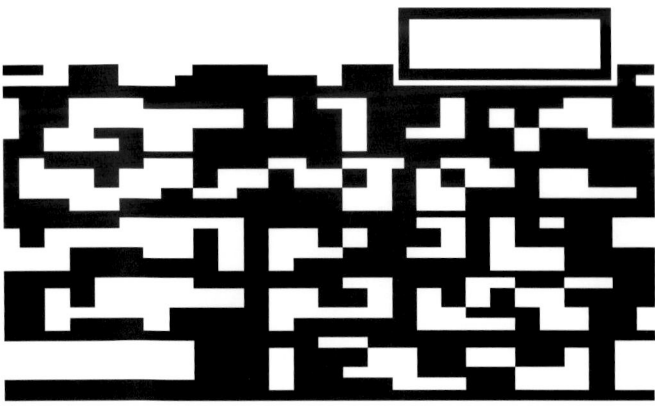

SERPENTE
CHAIR | RIO DE JANEIRO
Planning stage
Material: Wood / Prototype: Corian

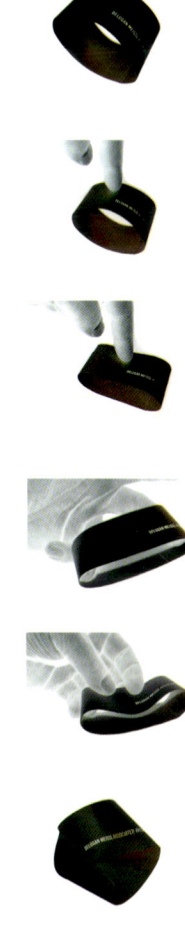

The chair incorporates the different parameters of dynamics, movement, body language, ergonomics and comfort and was created during a period of exploration of the material Corian. The aim was to develop coherent forms and contents beyond its established field of application and to lend the at first sight apparently brittle material an organic shape. Further development of the chair envisages the mould to be made out of wood or a lightweight plastic.

A band tied in the shape of a ring serves as formal starting point. The purposeful shaping of one side results in the seat, armrests and backrest. The origin's simplicity generates the piece's complexity, although its roots and immanent movement remain visible at all times. Together with its filigree feet the chair cleverly embodies the statement that is expressed by its static and dynamic purpose and forcefully articulates that which is also asserted in its name: Serpente.

Der in der Auseinandersetzung mit dem Werkstoff Corian entstandene Sessel inkorporiert die unterschiedlichen Parameter Dynamik, Bewegung, Körpersprache, Ergonomie und Komfort. Auch jenseits seiner bewährten Einsatzgebiete war es das Ziel, neue, schlüssige Formen und Inhalte zu entwickeln und das scheinbar optisch spröde Material in eine organische Gestalt zu transformieren. In der weiteren Entwicklung des Möbels soll die Formschale aus Holz oder einem leichten Kunststoff gefertigt werden.

Als formaler Ausgangspunkt dient ein ringförmig verknüpftes Band, das durch eine gezielte Verformung einer Seite, Sitzfläche, Arm- und Rückenlehne herausbildet. Aus der Einfachheit des Ursprungs generiert sich die Komplexität des Sitzmöbels, dessen Ausgangsform und immanente Bewegung stets ablesbar bleiben. Damit trägt der Sessel in Verbindung mit den bewusst filigran gehaltenen Füßen seiner statischen und dynamischen Bestimmung gekonnt Rechnung und bringt konsequent zum Ausdruck, was sich auch im Namen manifestiert: Serpente.

Le fauteuil incorpore différents paramètres – dynamique, mouvement, langage corporel, ergonomie et confort. Il est issu d'une confrontation avec une matière, le Corian. L'objectif des architectes, par-delà les utilisations conventionnelles, était de développer des formes et des contenus nouveaux et décisifs, et, par ailleurs, de transformer la raideur de cette matière en une création organique. Dans les versions ultérieures du meuble, la coque moulée sera fabriquée en bois ou dans un plastique léger.

La tige annulaire qui tient lieu de point de départ formel est déformée d'un côté, se muant ainsi en un siège, des bras et un dossier. La complexité du meuble, dont la forme originelle et le mouvement immanent restent toujours lisibles, découle de la simplicité de son origine. Ainsi, le siège, avec ses pieds filigranés, tient résolument compte de sa vocation statique et dynamique et exprime avec conséquence ce qui, du reste, est annoncé par son nom : Serpente.

El sillón integra diferentes parámetros como dinámica, movimiento, lenguaje corporal, ergonomía y comodidad. Es producto de la experimentación con el material Corian. El objetivo era desarrollar nuevas formas lógicas y contenidos que fueran más allá de las aplicaciones ya conocidas, así como transformar el material de apariencia áspera en una figura orgánica. En el desarrollo ulterior del mueble se ha de realizar la moldura de madera u otro plástico ligero.

Como punto de partida formal sirvió una banda enlazada en forma de anillo, que mediante una determinada conformación daba lugar a un lateral, el asiento, los brazos y el respaldo. De la simplicidad del origen surge la complejidad del asiento cuya forma de partida y su movimiento inmanente son legibles en todo momento. Así el sillón junto con las patas, a las que se ha dado conscientemente un aspecto de filigrana, cumple de modo magistral su designio estático y dinámico, y expresa consecuentemente lo que también manifiesta con su nombre: serpente.

Questa poltrona contiene in sé i diversi parametri di dinamicità, movimento, linguaggio fisico, ergonomia e comodità. È stata realizzata durante lo studio del materiale corian. Lo scopo era di creare nuove forme e contenuti, anche oltre ai suoi modi d'impiego provati, e di trasformare una materia apparentemente intrattabile in una forma organica. In un'ulteriore evoluzione il guscio verrà fabbricato in legno o in un materiale sintetico leggero.

Formale punto di partenza è un nastro a forma di anello: dalla deformazione di un lato si sviluppano sedile, bracciolo e schienale. Dalla semplicità dell'origine si genera la complessità della poltrona, ma la forma di partenza e il moto immanente rimangono sempre leggibili. Così, insieme ai suoi piedi consapevolmente tenuti fini, la poltrona tiene conto della sua destinazione statica e dinamica ed esprime con coerenza ciò che si manifesta anche nel nome: Serpente.

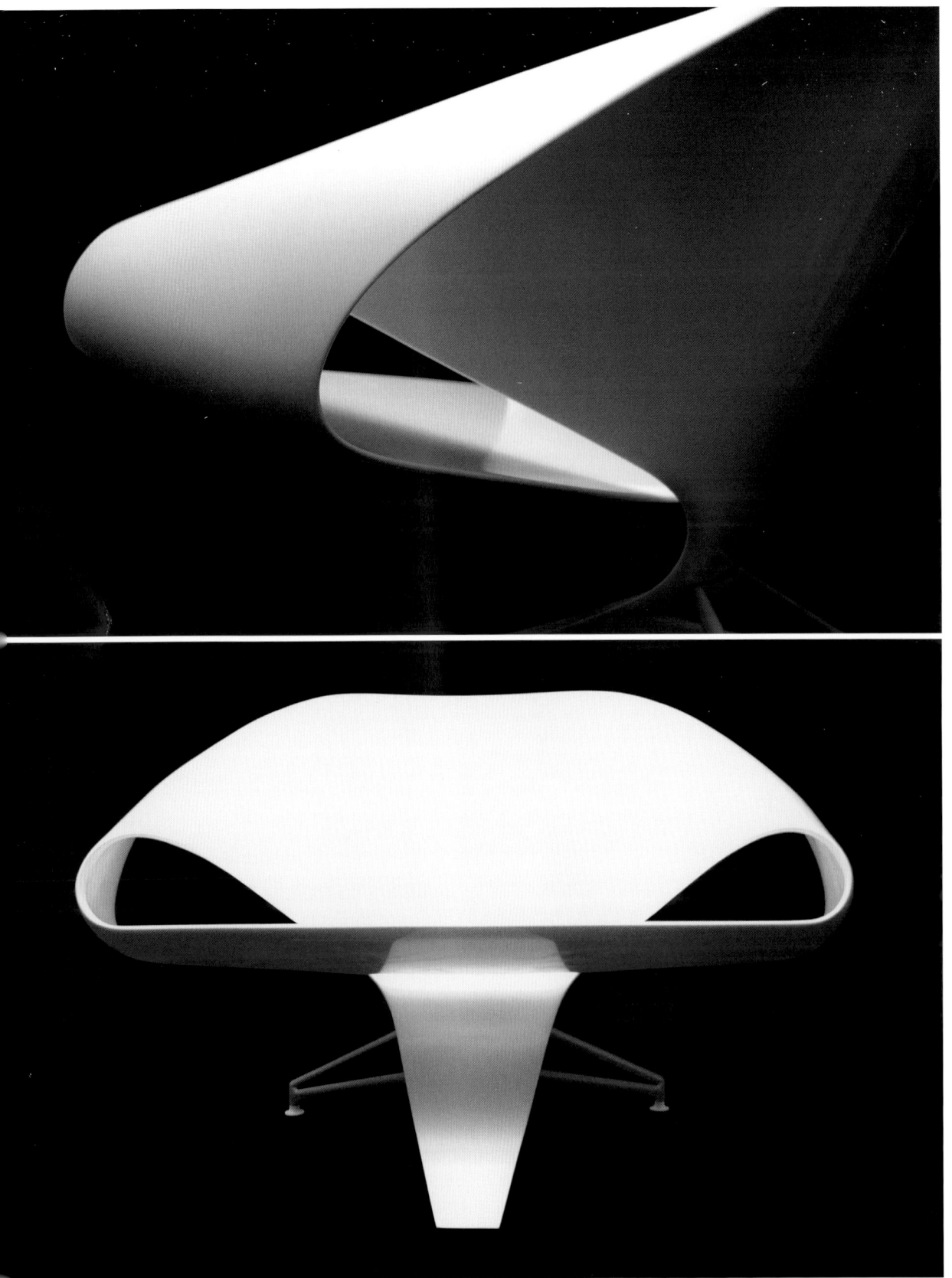

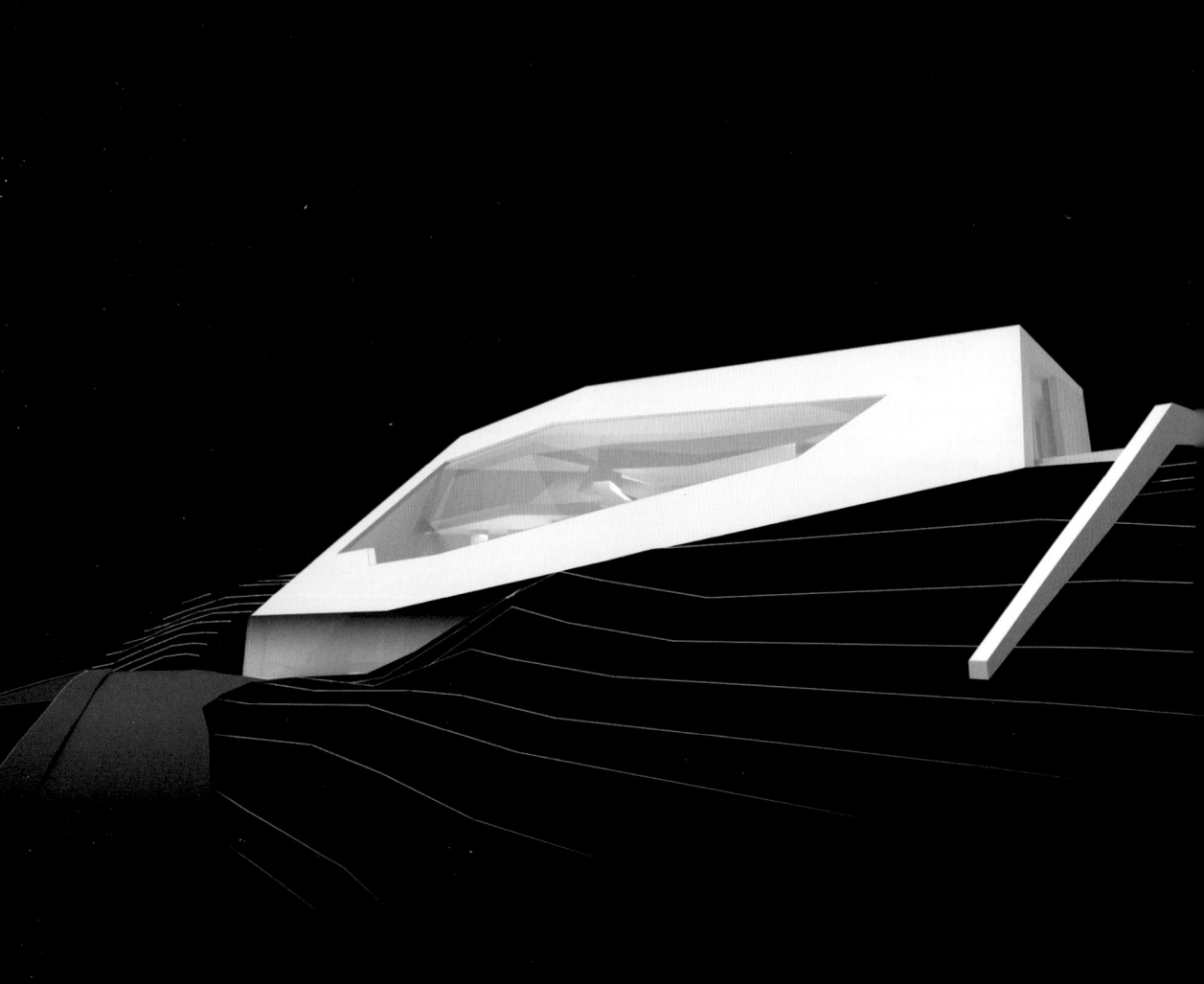

HOUSE H-L

SINGLE FAMILY HOUSE | VIENNA
Client: Private
Construction period: 2006-2007
Site area: 578 m^2
Floor area: 263 m^2

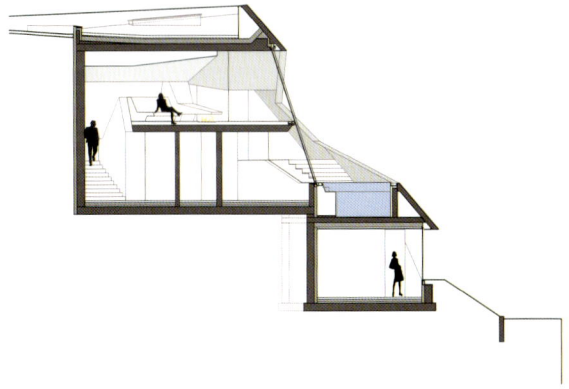

The extreme hillside situation of the designated property serves as the key design parameter and is also a space-defining feature of the building structure. The single-family house inserts itself deep into the slope which thus also becomes the living space. Only the striking streetside façade is exposed to public view. A frame, encircling the front of the building like a shield, protectively hides the internal functions which extend at varying levels into the hillside. This frame also incorporates outdoor areas located in front of the house, such as the swimming pool and terraces. The internal path through the building traces the extreme slope of the property over the various levels and plateaus. The natural environment thus becomes a ubiquitously perceptible aspect of living, and the internal paths take the exposed situation into consideration with a sweeping view of the viennese hinterland.

Die extreme Hanglage des zu bebauenden Grundstücks ist wesentlicher Entwurfsparameter und raumbildendes Charakteristikum der Gebäudestruktur. Das Einfamilienhaus schiebt sich tief in den Hang hinein, wodurch dieser gleichermaßen zum Lebensraum wird. Lediglich die einprägsame straßenseitige Fassade offenbart sich der Öffentlichkeit. Ein umlaufender Rahmen umfasst schildartig die Gebäudefront und beherbergt die internen Funktionen, die sich über eine differenzierte Höhenentwicklung auf das Hanginnere erstrecken. Der Rahmen bezieht auch die vor dem Haus liegenden Freiraumbereiche wie Schwimmbad und Terrassen mit ein. Die Wegeführung innerhalb des Gebäudes vollzieht über Niveausprünge und Plateaus das starke Grundstücksgefälle nach. Die natürliche Umgebung wird zum allgegenwärtigen erlebbaren Aspekt des Wohnens und kann bei einem weit reichenden Blick ins Wiener Umland genossen werden.

La déclivité extrême du terrain à bâtir est un paramètre essentiel du projet et une caractéristique génératrice d'espace de la structure de la maison. Celle-ci s'insère profondément dans cette pente qui devient ainsi espace de vie. Seule l'impressionnante façade sur la rue s'ouvre au public. Le cadre continu qui l'entoure, tel un bouclier, cache les fonctions internes qui se poursuivent sur l'intérieur de la pente à travers les différents niveaux. Le cadre englobe également les aires de loisirs situées devant la maison, comme la piscine et les terrasses. Le cheminement à l'intérieur de la demeure suit la forte déclivité du terrain grâce à des écarts de niveaux et des plateaux. L'environnement naturel devient un aspect indissociable de l'habitat, que le panorama sur les environs de Vienne permet d'apprécier.

La extrema inclinación del terreno se convierte en el parámetro esencial del diseño y es la característica constructiva de la estructura del edificio. La vivienda unifamiliar se introduce profundamente en la pendiente que de este modo pasa a convertirse en espacio vital. La expresiva fachada de la calle es el único elemento que se muestra al público. Un marco continuo envuelve como un escudo el frente del edificio y resguarda las funciones internas, que se prolongan hacia el interior de la pendiente mediante una evolución diferenciada de alturas. El marco engloba también las zonas exteriores de la casa como la piscina y las terrazas. El itinerario interior del edificio reproduce sobre diferencias de nivel y plataformas la fuerte inclinación del terreno. El entorno natural se convierte en aspecto omnipresente de la vivienda, que se puede disfrutar con la amplia panorámica de los alrededores de Viena.

L'estrema pendenza del terreno da edificare è parametro fondamentale per la progettazione e caratteristica creatrice di spazi nella struttura della costruzione. La casa unifamiliare si spinge profondamente nel pendio che diventa così spazio vitale. Solo l'impressionante facciata sul lato della strada si presenta al pubblico. Una cornice circonda come uno scudo la facciata dell'edificio e contiene le funzioni interne, che si estendono fino all'interno del pendio in un differenziato sviluppo di livelli. La cornice include anche gli spazi esterni con piscina e terrazze. I percorsi all'interno dell'edificio seguono la forte inclinazione del terreno con differenze di livello e plateaus. L'ambiente circostante naturale diviene parte integrante della casa e può essere apprezzato alla vista dell'esteso panorama sui dintorni di Vienna.

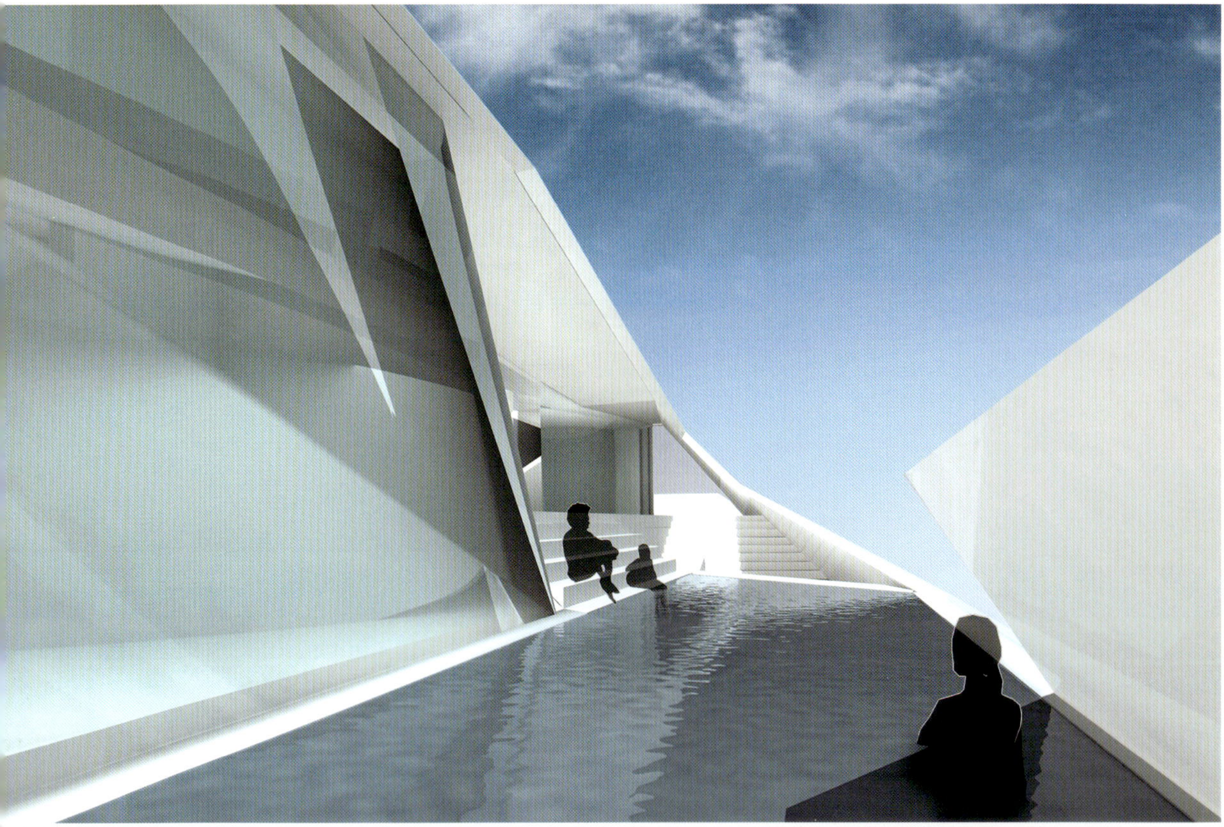

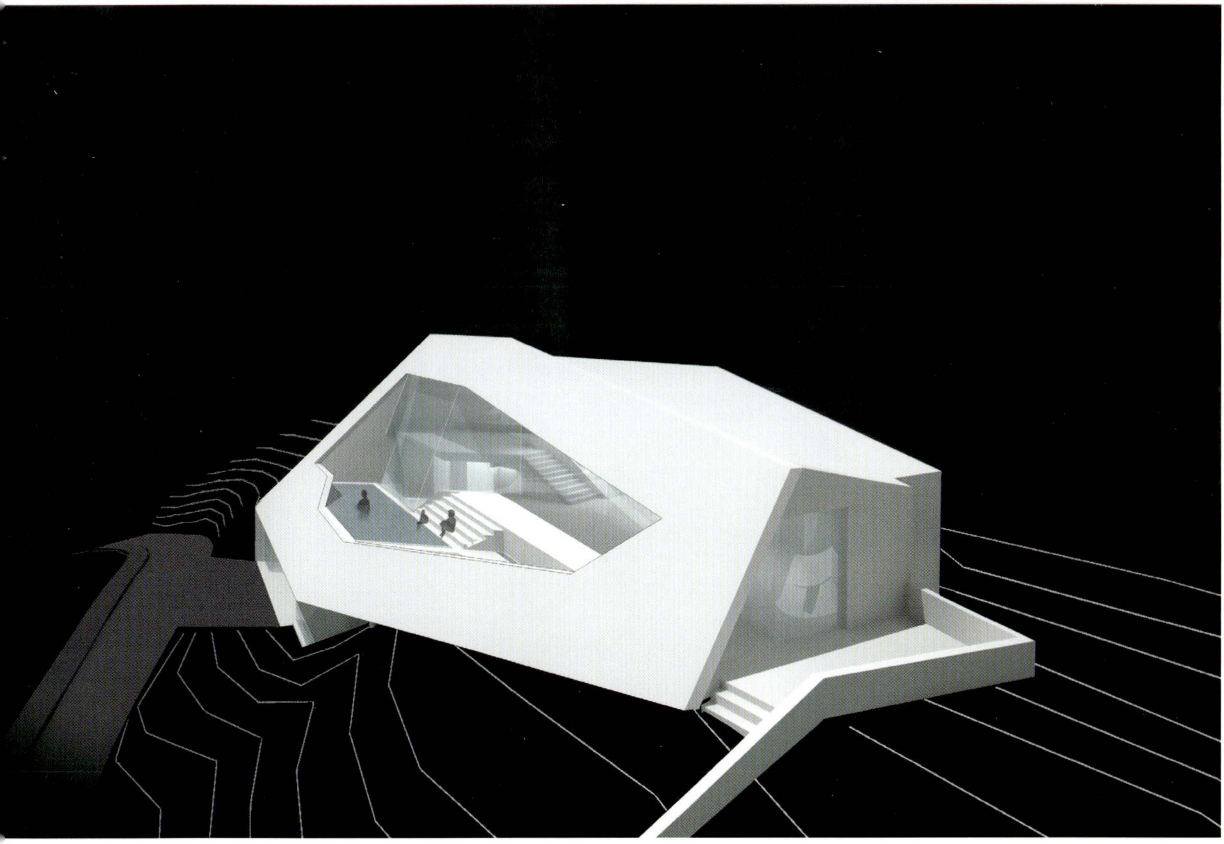

PORSCHE

PORSCHE MUSEUM STUTTGART
Competition: 1st Prize
Client: Porsche AG, Stuttgart
Construction period: 2005-2007
Exhibition area: 5.000 m²
Floor area: 13.253 m²
Visualizations: Delugan Meissl, Porsche AG

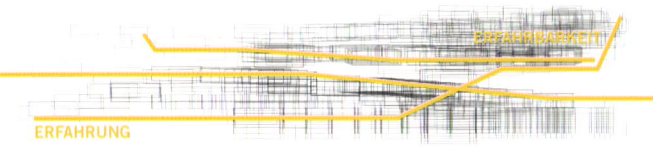

ERFAHRUNG

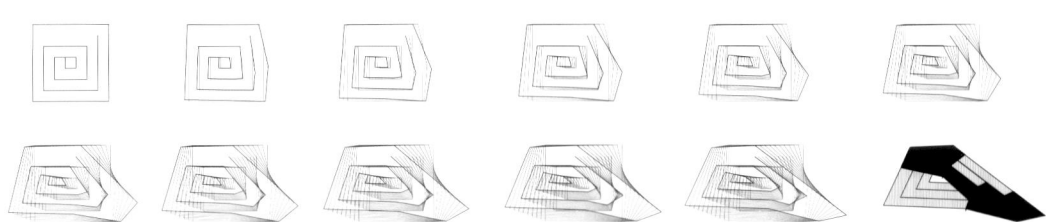

The new Porsche Museum will create a space for lending architectural expression to the company's self-confident stance and high standards, while at the same time properly expressing Porsche's dynamic vitality.

Conceived as a gravity-defying and dynamically formed structure, the museum seems to hover above the folded topography of the ground level. The monolith contains the exhibition area and provides the spatial potential for experiencing the "Porsche cosmos." The entrance area of the building's basis not only acts as a foyer and hub but also gives interesting insight into the vintage car workshop and the archive. The exhibition space has been configured as a vast arena that rises like a spiral and renounces hierarchical principles of order as well as a linear, predetermined single approach of presentation. Because the spiral's nature is first of all pure system of ways, it is extended and transformed in order to create different zones. Various relations are assembled in a flexible way around its organizing center. Cross references emerge and can be followed in both a spatial and thematic sense.

Mit dem neuen Porschemuseum wird ein Ort geschaffen, der der selbstbewussten Haltung und dem hohen Anspruch des Unternehmens architektonisch Ausdruck verleiht und zugleich seiner Dynamik Rechnung trägt.

Als vom Boden losgelöster, dynamisch geformter Körper scheint das Museum über der gefalteten Topographie des Erdgeschossniveaus zu schweben. Der Monolith birgt den Ausstellungsraum in sich und gibt der Erfahrbarkeit des „Kosmos Porsche" Raum. Der Eingangsbereich in der Gebäudebasis fungiert nicht nur als Foyer und Verteiler, sondern eröffnet gleichzeitig interessante Einblicke in den Werkstattbereich und das Archiv. Der Ausstellungsraum ist als weitläufige, spiralförmig ansteigende Arena konzipiert. Auf ein hierarchisches Ordnungsprinzip und eine linear vorgegebene, einzige Zugangsweise der Darstellung wird verzichtet. Da die Spiralform ihrem Wesen nach zunächst reines Wegesystem ist, wird sie gestreckt und transformiert, um unterschiedliche Zonen herauszubilden. Verschiedene Beziehungen bauen sich flexibel um den organisierenden Mittelpunkt der Spirale auf. Querverweise werden offenbar und lassen sich in der räumlichen und inhaltlichen Verknüpfung nachvollziehen.

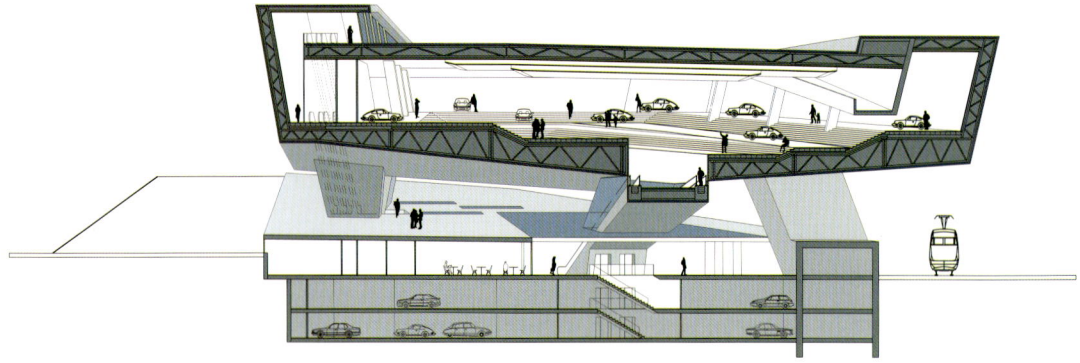

Le nouveau musée Porsche se veut un lieu conférant une expression architectonique au prestige et aux exigences de l'entreprise, tout en tenant compte de sa dynamique.

Le musée semble flotter au-dessus de la topographie plissée du rez-de-chaussée, comme un corps de forme dynamique et soulevé de terre. Le monolithe qui abrite l'espace d'exposition offre au visiteur la possibilité de faire l'expérience de « l'univers Porsche ». La base du bâtiment où se trouve l'entrée fonctionne, à l'intérieur, non seulement comme hall et distributeur, mais donne en même temps des aperçus sur la zone des ateliers et les archives. L'espace d'exposition est conçu comme une vaste arène qui s'organise en spirale ascendante. On a renoncé à un principe d'ordre hiérarchique, ainsi qu'à imposer un mode de pénétration unique et linéaire. La forme en spirale étant par essence un pur système de déambulation avant tout, elle s'étire et se transforme pour constituer différentes zones. Plusieurs relations s'établissent en souplesse autour du point central et organisateur de la spirale, les références se font jour et deviennent parfaitement compréhensibles dans la jonction spatiale et substantielle.

Con el nuevo museo Porsche se ha creado un lugar que expresa arquitectónicamente la actitud segura y las grandes aspiraciones de la empresa tomando a la vez en consideración la dinámica de Porsche.

Como si fuera un cuerpo suelto y dinámicamente formado, el museo parece flotar sobre la sinuosa topografía de la planta baja. El monolito alberga la sala de exposición y proporciona un espacio para experimentar el "universo Porsche". La base del edificio contiene la zona de entrada y no sólo hace de vestíbulo y distribuidor, también permite echar una ojeada a la zona de talleres y al archivo. La sala de exposición está concebida como un amplio estadio, dispuesto en forma de espiral ascendente. Se ha prescindido de un orden jerárquico y también de mostrar un único modo de acceso lineal y prescrito. Como por naturaleza la espiral es ante todo un puro sistema itinerario, ésta se extiende y transforma para crear distintas zonas. En torno al centro organizativo de la espiral se construyen de modo flexible diferentes relaciones, se descubren referencias y se dejan reproducir en el enlace espacial y sustancial.

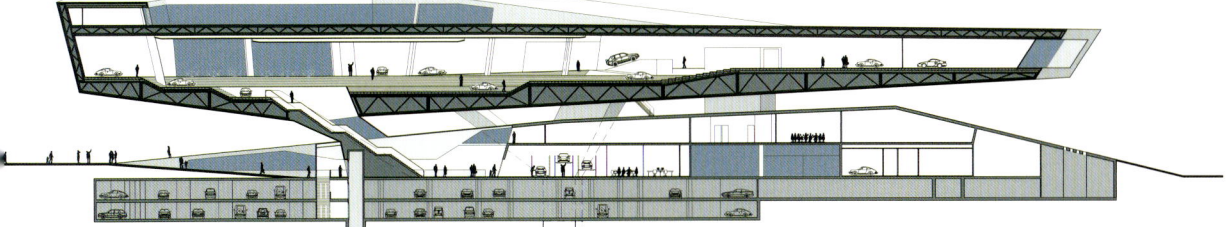

Con il nuovo Museo Porsche si vuole realizzare un luogo che esprima architettonicamente l'atteggiamento orgoglioso ed esigente dell'impresa e allo stesso tempo tenga conto della dinamicità della Porsche.

Il museo sembra fluttuare sulla topografia ripiegata del piano terra come un corpo dinamico staccato dal terreno. Il monolito racchiude la sala d'esposizione e crea uno spazio per percepire il "cosmo Porsche". La base dell'edificio contiene l'ingresso e funge all'interno non solo come foyer e punto di smistamento, ma concede contemporaneamente uno sguardo nell'officina e nell'archivio. La sala espositiva è concepita come un'ampia arena che, salendo, si sviluppa a spirale. Si rinuncia ad un sistema di ordini gerarchici e al mostrare singoli ingressi linearmente premeditati. La forma a spirale, che per sua natura rappresenta un tragitto, si allunga e si trasforma per creare spazi diversi. Intorno al centro organizzatore della spirale si formano in modo flessibile delle relazioni differenti. I richiami nel collegamento spaziale e contenutistico diventano ovvi e comprensibili.

SIMPLY 11
BUSINESSPARK | VIENNA
Address: Modecenterstraße 17-19, 1110 Vienna
Client: Gobiet & Partner ZT Gmbh, Vienna
Construction period: 2006-2008
Site area: 18 ha
Floor area: 37.852 m^2
Visualizations: Schreiner, Kastler

As part of a new city development area former business premises in Vienna will be converted to a new business park. The area's strength lies in its optimal infrastructure and access to public transport and road network. The project conceptualises five structures along a boulevardesque feeder flanked by public spaces. The free geometrical layout and resulting angles of the structures create a variety of different spatial situations and visual relationships in connection to its environment. The areas in between boast extensive greenery and offer thus great relaxing and leisure qualities. The entrances to the units can all be accessed from the boulevard. If necessary, single buildings may be connected by footbridges to form larger units. A single storey structure is to form the base of the former Schlachthausbahn railway line which is to be opened up for pedestrians and cyclists. It enters the business park from the South and connects the two southernmost units. The base could be home to a variety of businesses or showrooms etc.

Auf einem ehemaligen Firmengelände in Wien entsteht im Zuge eines neuen städtischen Entwicklungsareals ein neuer Businesspark. Die Stärke des Gebiets liegt in der optimalen Anbindung an die öffentlichen Verkehrsmittel und das übergeordnete Straßennetz. Der Entwurf sieht fünf Baukörper entlang einer boulevardartigen Erschließungsfläche vor, die von öffentlichen Nutzungen flankiert ist. Durch die freie geometrische Anordnung und Winkelbildung der Baukörper ergeben sich abwechslungsreiche Raumsituationen und Blickbeziehungen zur Umgebung. Die Zwischenräume sind großflächig begrünt und bieten somit eine hohe Aufenthaltsqualität. Die Eingangsbereiche der einzelnen *units* liegen direkt am Boulevard. Einzelne Gebäude können bei Bedarf mittels Verbindungsbrücken zu größeren Einheiten verknüpft werden. Ein eingeschossiger Sockel führt das Dammniveau der südlichen Schlachthausbahn, die zukünftig als Fuß- und Radweg genutzt werden kann, nach Norden in das Plangebiet hinein und verbindet die beiden südlichen Einheiten miteinander. Im Sockelinneren sind Geschäftsnutzungen, showrooms oder ähnliches denkbar.

Un centre d'affaires est en train de voir le jour à Vienne sur un ancien terrain industriel, dans le cadre d'une nouvelle zone de développement urbain. Le point fort du terrain se situe dans les liaisons optimales avec les transports en commun et le réseau routier. Le projet concerne cinq ouvrages le long d'une aire de mise en valeur similaire à un boulevard, flanquée de services publics. La disposition géométrique libre et la forme angulaire des bâtiments permettent de varier les situations spatiales et les relations optiques avec l'environnement. Les espaces intermédiaires sont largement végétalisés, offrant une qualité de vie élevée. Les halls d'entrée des différentes unités s'ouvrent sur le boulevard. En cas de nécessité, il est possible de relier quelques bâtiments par des passerelles pour former de plus grandes unités. Un socle d'un étage introduit au niveau de la chaussée la partie sud d'une rue, la Schlachthausbahn, que pourront utiliser à l'avenir les piétons et les cyclistes, vers le nord dans le terrain à construire, et relie les deux unités orientées au sud. Ce socle pourrait accueillir des commerces, showrooms ou autres.

Dentro de una nueva área de desarrollo urbanística se crea un nuevo centro de negocios en el solar de una antigua empresa de Viena. La principal ventaja de la zona reside en que está comunicada de forma óptima por los medios de transporte públicos y por la principal red viaria. El diseño prevé cinco cuerpos arquitectónicos a lo largo de una superficie de infraestructuras tipo boulevard, flanqueada por servicios públicos. La ordenación libre y geométrica de los inmuebles y su disposición en ángulo da lugar a situaciones espaciales variables y a diferentes perspectivas del entorno. Entre los edificios se disponen grandes superficies verdes que ofrecen así una calidad de vida de alto nivel. Las entradas de cada unit dan al boulevard. Si fuera necesario se puede enlazar los edificios aislados con las unidades grandes mediante puentes de unión. El terraplén del ferrocarril del matadero meridional, que en un futuro podrá utilizarse como carril de bicicletas o vía peatonal, se introduce hacia el norte hasta el área planificada mediante una base de un piso de altura y enlaza entre sí las dos unidades del sur. En el interior del zócalo se podría instalar comercios o showrooms.

Su un terreno dove un tempo si trovava una ditta, a Vienna, in una nuova area di sviluppo urbano, sta nascendo un nuovo centro affari. Il vantaggio della zona consiste nell'ottima raggiungibilità sia con i mezzi di trasporto pubblici che dalla rete stradale principale. Il progetto prevede cinque edifici lungo uno spazio di accessi a forma di viale, affiancato da spazi ad uso pubblico. Grazie alla libera disposizione geometrica e agli angoli tra le costruzioni, si creano molteplici situazioni spaziali e relazioni visuali con l'ambiente circostante. Gli spazi non costruiti sono molto verdi e in questo modo offrono un'alta qualità di permanenza. Gli ingressi delle singole unità si affacciano sul viale. In caso di bisogno i singoli edifici possono essere collegati tra di loro attraverso passerelle e formare così unità più grandi. Un fabbricato di un piano unico porta il rialzamento della ferrovia proveniente da sud, la Schlachthausbahn, che in futuro potrà essere usata come passaggio pedonale e ciclabile, verso nord nell'area del progetto e collega le due unità poste a sud. L'interno della base può essere adibito a negozi o showroom.

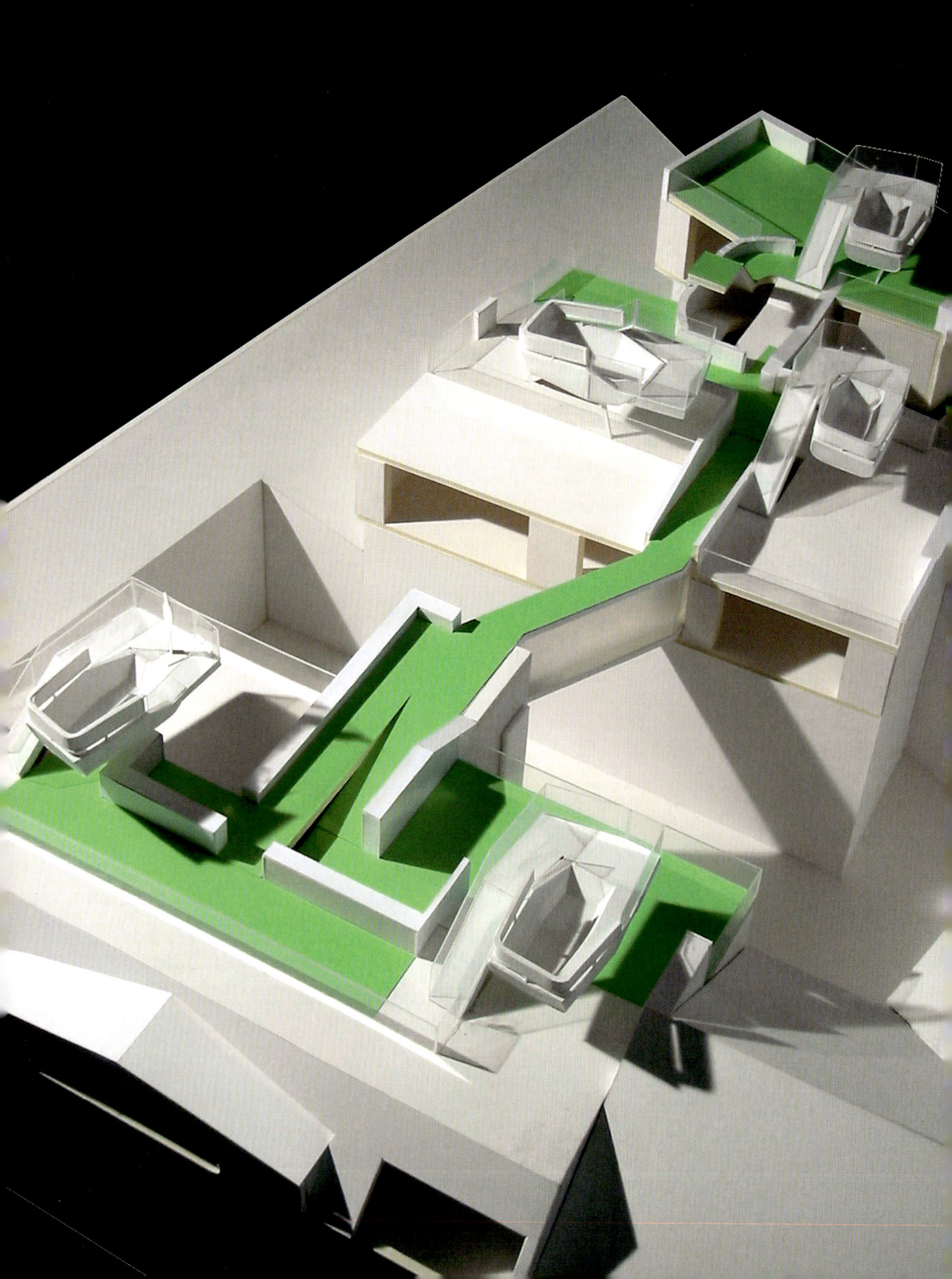

APARTMENTS FLEISCHMARKT
ROOFTOP EXPANSION | VIENNA
Client: Guttmann GmbH, Vienna
Construction period: 2006-2008
Floor area: 594 m^2
Terraces: 116 m^2

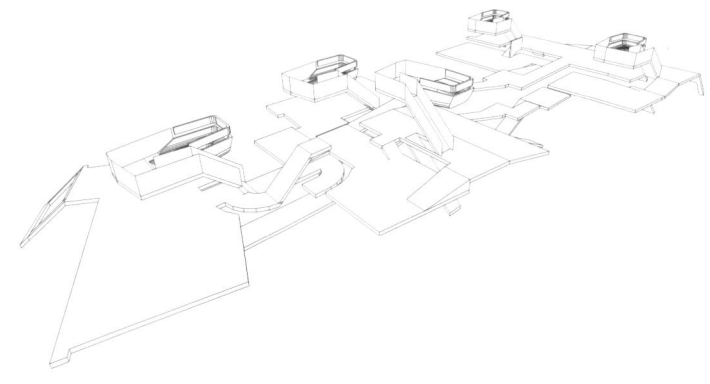

A loft extension of two adjacent buildings in Vienna's first district results in five generously sized apartments. The buildings are connected via footbridges and a central lift grants access to the units. The apartments have a spacious loft-style character and both furnishings and functionality greatly exceed current standards: the forms resulting from the overall architectural context include seating possibilities, divan and resting areas as well as luxurious bathing suites with whirlpools. The furnishing arrangement achieves a variety of different spatial qualities and underlines the generous and fluid impression of space. Upstairs there are ample private roof decks with wooden planks as floorings and plenty of green. The architecture responds to the special location by combining a very high quality of life and leisure time with the spectacular views on the protected first district of Vienna including St. Stephen's Cathedral. It thus positions itself where only the sky is the limit.

Fünf großzügige Apartments entstehen durch den Dachbodenausbau zweier benachbarter Gebäude im ersten Wiener Bezirk. Die Gebäudeteile werden durch Stege miteinander verbunden und von einem zentralen Lift aus erschlossen. Die Wohnungen zeichnen sich durch einen loftartigen Charakter aus – mit Möbeln und Nutzungsmöglichkeiten, die über den Standard weit hinausgehen: Die sich aus dem architektonischen Gesamtzusammenhang generierenden Formen beinhalten Sitzmöglichkeiten, Liegelandschaften sowie luxuriöse Badebereiche mit Whirlpools. Der Formen-verlauf des Mobiliars erzielt unterschiedliche räumliche Qualitäten und unterstreicht den großzügigen fließenden Raum-eindruck. Über den Apartments liegen private, weiträumige Dachterrassen, die mit einer Holzbeplankung und viel Grün versehen werden. Die Architektur reagiert auf die spezielle Lage, indem sie eine hohe Wohn- und Aufenthaltsqualität mit dem spektakulären Ausblick auf den denkmalgeschützten ersten Wiener Bezirk samt Stephansdom verbindet und sich dort zu positionieren weiß, wo der Himmel beginnt.

L'aménagement des combles de deux bâtiments voisins, dans le premier arrondissement de Vienne, a donné nais-sance à cinq généreux appartements. Les différentes parties, desservies par un ascenseur central, sont reliées les unes aux autres par des passerelles. Les appartements s'apparentent à de spacieux lofts. Le mobilier et les utilisations dépassent de loin l'aménagement standard : les formes générées par l'ensemble architectonique proposent des aires pour s'asseoir ou s'étendre, et des salles d'eau luxueuses équipées de baignoires à vagues. Le développement formel du mobilier se traduit par des qualités spatiales variées et souligne l'impression d'espace continu et fluide. Au-dessus des appartements, les vastes terrasses du toit sont habillées de bois et végétalisées. Cette architecture, qui unit une remarquable qualité d'habitation et de séjour à une vue spectaculaire sur la cathédrale Saint-Étienne et le premier arrondissement de Vienne, protégé pour sa valeur historique, répond au site exceptionnel et sait se positionner là où commence le ciel.

Al construir sobre los tejados de dos edificios contiguos del distrito I de Viena se crean cinco amplios apartamentos. Las diferentes partes del edificio comunican entre sí por medio de pasarelas y están conectadas por un ascensor central. Las viviendas se caracterizan por su gran amplitud tipo loft. Los muebles y las posibilidades de aprovecha-miento superan ampliamente los estándares: las formas originadas por la continuidad arquitectónica general incluyen diferentes tipos de asientos, zonas de descanso y lujosos baños con bañera de hidromasaje. El desarrollo formal del mobiliario está destinado a conseguir diferentes calidades espaciales y subraya la generosa sensación de espacio continuo. Sobre los apartamentos hay amplias azoteas privadas provistas de una cubierta de madera y mucho verde. En vista de la especial ubicación, la arquitectura reacciona aunando la espectacular panorámica del monumental distrito I de Viena, que incluye la catedral de San Esteban, con una elevada calidad habitacional y sabe tomar posiciones allí donde el cielo comienza.

Dall'ampliamento del sottotetto di due edifici vicini nel primo distretto di Vienna risultano cinque appartamenti di dimensioni generose. Le parti degli edifici sono collegate per mezzo di passerelle e accessibili attraverso un ascensore centrale. Gli appartamenti si distinguono per il loro carattere da loft. I mobili e le possibilità d'impiego superano di molto lo standard. Le forme create dal contesto architettonico generale contengono angoli per sedersi, spazi per distendersi e lussuosi bagni con idromassaggio. L'andamento delle forme dell'arredo realizza effetti spaziali diversi e sottolinea l'impressione di generosità e di fluidità dell'ambiente. Sopra gli appartamenti si trovano grandi terrazze private che sono rivestite di assi di legno e munite di molto verde. L'architettura reagisce alla posizione particolare, coniugando un'alta qualità di permanenza e di abitabilità con un panorama spettacolare sul primo distretto di Vienna – tutelato come patrimoniomio artistico – con il Stephansdom, e dimostrando così di sapersi collocare proprio dove inizia il cielo.

CASA INVISIBILIS
SINGLE FAMILY HOUSE / EXTENSION | VORARLBERG
Client: Private
Planning stage
Floor area: 73 m^2

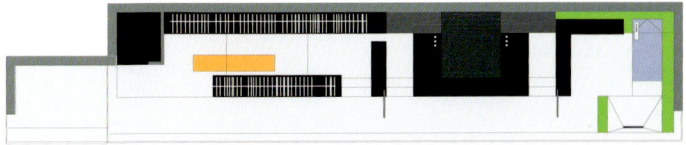

The site for the extension to a private contractor's existing building is situated in a remarkably heterogeneous environment: during the course of time numerous extensions and additions as well as outbuildings of different colours and materials have been added to the residence. The family's current plans include increasing the living space and integrating a new bedroom which is to function not only as a place of rest but also includes a large walk-in wardrobe. Delugan Meissl Associated Architects have worked on and found a solution which corresponds to the existing patchwork architecture: an unostentatious but elegant box now thrones on top of some existing buildings. The mirror-clad façade reflects its environment. The appearance of the new addition changes with the time of day (and year), its contours being more or less pronounced respectively. The extremes of a very clear and reduced architectural language are united with an almost irritating visual dissolution of the building. The part of the box which houses the bed displays a kind of double layer: movable elements enable the complete opening of both front wall and roof so one can sleep under the starry sky. Alternatively both surfaces can be protected with glass panels.

Der Bauplatz für die Gebäudeerweiterung eines privaten Bauherrn befindet sich in einem ausgesprochen heterogenen Umfeld: Der Residenz wurden im Laufe der Jahre verschiedene Zu- und Aufbauten sowie Solitärgebäude unterschiedlicher Farbe und Materialität hinzugefügt. Nun plant die Familie den Wohnbereich zu vergrößern und einen neuen Schlafraum zu integrieren, der nicht nur als Ruhezone fungiert, sondern auch einen großzügigen, begehbaren Schrank beinhaltet. Delugan Meissl Associated Architects haben eine Lösung erarbeitet, die mit der existenten Patchwork Architektur korrespondiert: Eine schlichte, wenngleich elegante Box, thront nun auf einigen der vorhandenen Gebäude. Die spiegelverkleidete Fassade reflektiert die Umgebung. Während des Tages- und Jahresverlaufs ändert sich das Erscheinungsbild der Aufstockung und ihre Konturen treten mehr oder weniger stark hervor. Die Extreme einer sehr klaren und reduzierten Architektursprache werden mit einer geradezu irritierenden visuellen „Auflösung" des Gebäudes vereint. Der Teil der Box, in dem das Bett steht, weist eine Art doppelte Schicht auf: Dank flexibler Elemente können die vordere Wand und das Dach geschlossen bleiben oder zum Schlafen unter freiem Himmel sowohl komplett geöffnet als auch wahlweise mit einem Glasschutz versehen werden.

Le site prévu pour l'extension de cette résidence privée correspond à un environnement des plus hétérogènes : au fil des ans, divers éléments s'y sont adjoints ou surajoutés, ainsi que des bâtiments isolés, de différentes couleurs et matières. Aujourd'hui, la famille souhaite agrandir l'espace habitable et installer une nouvelle chambre qui doit fonctionner non seulement comme zone de repos, mais comprendre aussi un vaste dressing. Delugan Meissl Associated Architects ont élaboré une solution qui répond à cette architecture en patchwork : un cube sobre et élégant trône sur l'une des constructions existantes. La façade revêtue de miroirs reflète l'environnement. Au fil de la journée (et de l'année), l'apparence de la structure et ses contours s'affirment ou s'effacent. Les extrêmes d'un langage architectural très clair et concis s'unissent à une « dissolution » visuelle tout à fait déroutante de la maison. La partie du cube qui abrite le lit révèle une sorte de double strate : grâce à des éléments flexibles, la paroi avant et le toit peuvent se fermer ou, au contraire, s'ouvrir complètement si les propriétaires souhaitent dormir à la belle étoile, ou bien encore recevoir, le cas échéant une protection vitrée.

La ampliación de edificio encargada por un cliente privado se encuentra en un contexto francamente heterogéneo; a lo largo de los años la residencia se ha sometido a diferentes reformas y ampliaciones y se le han añadido construcciones aisladas de distintos colores y materiales. La familia planea ahora ampliar el espacio habitable incorporando un nuevo dormitorio que además de servir de zona de descanso, habrá de incluir un espacioso armario empotrado. Delugan Meissl Associated Architects ha desarrollado una solución que guarda relación con la arquitectura patchwork ya existente. Una caja sencilla y elegante a la vez, se alza ahora sobre algunos de los edificios ya existentes. La fachada revestida de espejo refleja el entorno. La apariencia externa del edificio, cuyos contornos resaltan con mayor o menor intensidad, va cambiando con el transcurso del día (y del año). Los extremos de un lenguaje arquitectónico muy claro y reducido se aúnan con una "disolución" visual del edificio claramente desconcertante. La parte de la caja que alberga la cama presenta una especie de doble capa; elementos flexibles permiten mantener cerrados la pared delantera y el techo, abrirlos por completo si se desea dormir a cielo abierto, o adaptarles una cubierta de cristal.

L'area dedicata all'ampliamento dell'edificio di un committente privato si trova in un ambito del tutto eterogeneo: nel corso degli anni alla residenza sono state aggiunte varie sopraelevazioni, dépendance e costruzioni indipendenti, di colori e materiali diversi. Ora la famiglia ha intenzione di ampliare il soggiorno e di aggiungere una nuova camera da letto, che, oltre a essere un luogo di riposo, comprenda anche un guardaroba di generose dimensioni. Delugan Meissl Associated Architects hanno studiato una soluzione che tiene conto dell'architettura patchwork esistente. Un semplice, ma elegante box troneggia adesso su alcuni degli edifici presenti. La facciata rivestita di specchi riflette l'ambiente circostante. L'aspetto dell'annesso cambia nel corso della giornata (e dell'anno), variando le linee di contorno. Gli estremi di un linguaggio architettonico molto chiaro e minimalistico vengono uniti ad un'irritante "dissoluzione" visuale dell'edificio. La parte del box che alloggia il letto dispone di una specie di doppio rivestimento: grazie a elementi flessibili, la parete anteriore e il tetto possono restare chiusi o, per dormire a cielo aperto, essere sia spalancati del tutto, sia rivestiti facoltativamente di una protezione in vetro.

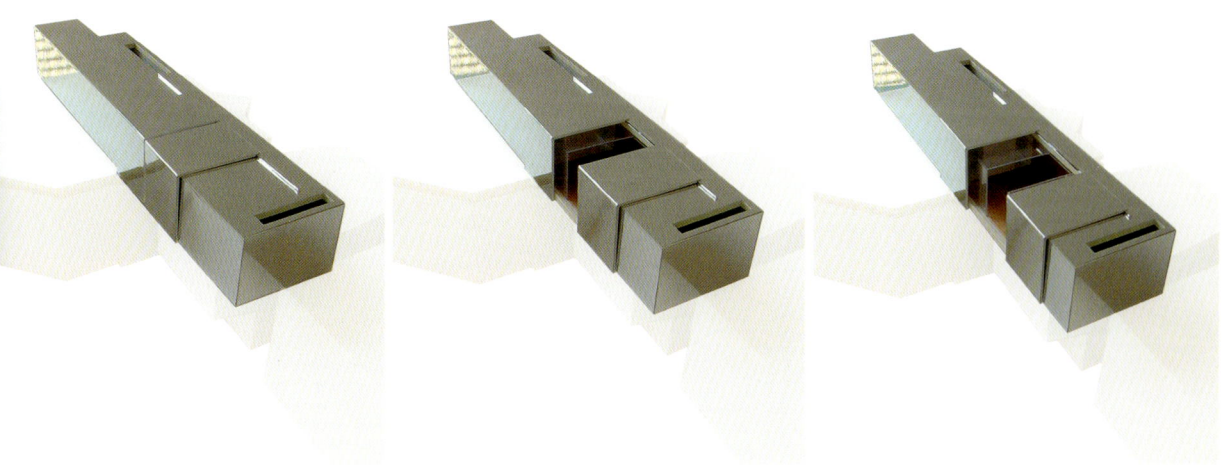

FILM MUSEUM AMSTERDAM
Competition: 1st Prize
Client: Filmmuseum Amsterdam
Project development: ING Real Estate
Construction period: 2006-2009
Gross floor space: 8.200 m^2
Floor area: 5.700 m^2

As a free standing sculpture, the film museum is situated on an exposed site opposite the old part of the city and the Central Station, right on a bend of the IJ. It functions as an outstanding landmark of the new urban development in the north of Amsterdam. Its horizontal, dynamic entity acts as a complement to the neighbouring Shell Tower. As a weightless configuration the crystalline geometry changes perpetually its appearance in the shifting play of light. To approach the Museum from the city center is to experience a suspenseful "dramaturgy" of differing spatial and visual sequences. Therefore the film museum to some extent pays tribute to the parameters of motion and light that are especially relevant to the medium of film. These endow the building with its identity while enhancing the perception and experience of it on this specific site. The sweeping central "arena" serves as the spatial and functional focal point and represents an interface between the exterior space and the various internal functions. It thereby acts simultaneously as light-infused meeting point, stage, rest area, vista platform, bar, café, restaurant and living space.

exhibition
arena
terrace
cinema
offices
exhibition
arena
terrace
extroverted
introverted

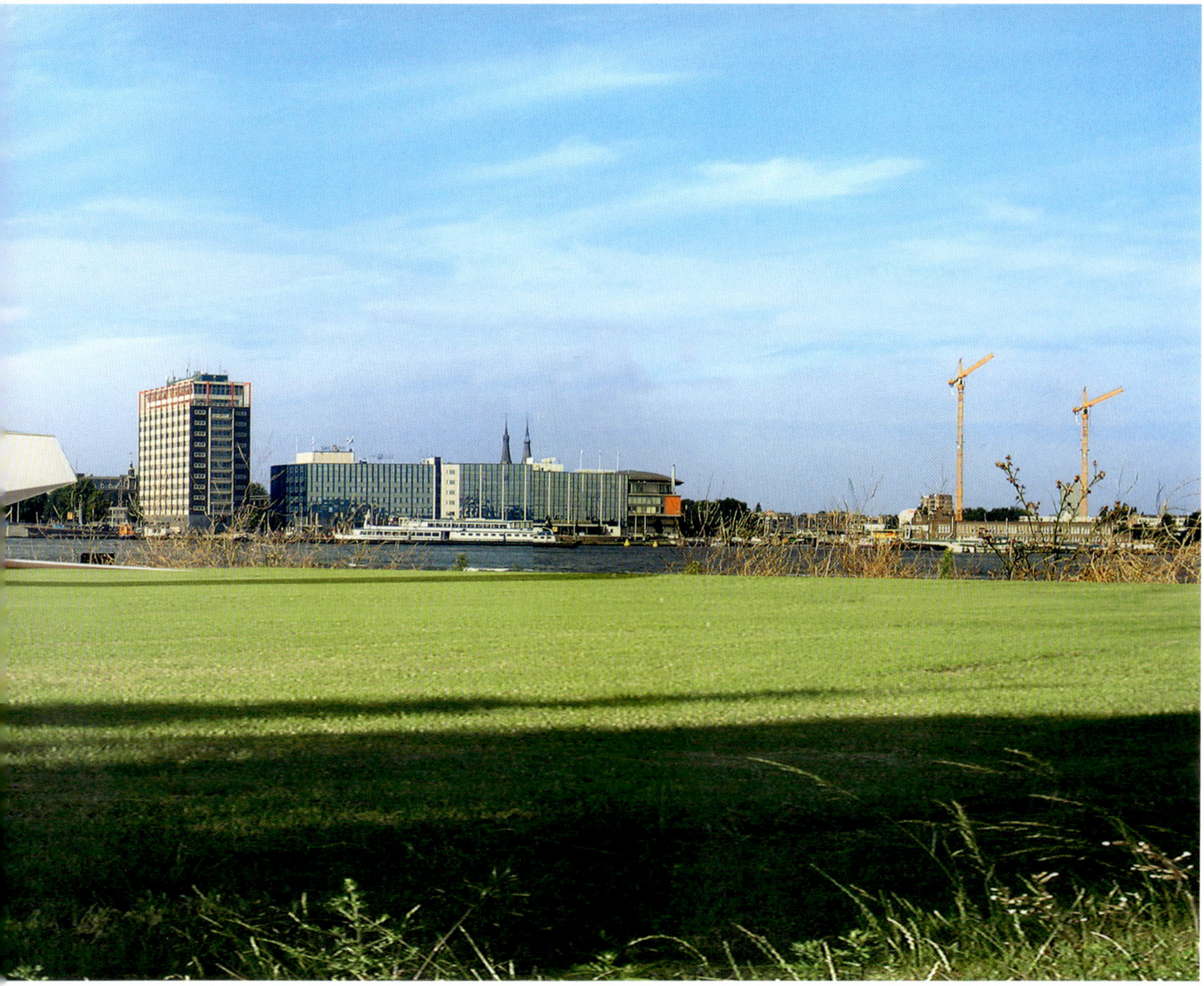

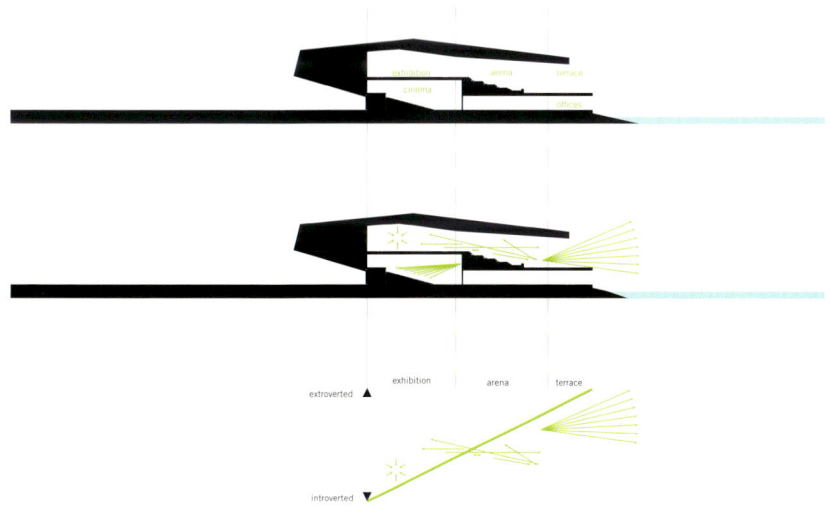

Als freistehende Skulptur befindet sich das Filmmuseum in exponierter Lage gegenüber Altstadt und Hauptbahnhof, direkt an einer Uferbiegung der IJ. Hier ist es weithin sichtbares Zeichen für ein neues Stadtentwicklungsgebiet im Amsterdamer Norden. Sein horizontal ausgerichteter, dynamischer Körper bildet eine Ergänzung zum benachbarten Shellturm. Im wechselnden Spiel der Lichtverhältnisse tritt die kristalline Geometrie als leichte Konfiguration immer wieder anders in Erscheinung. Die Annäherung an das Gebäude aus Richtung Innenstadt, entspricht einer spannend inszenierten Dramaturgie mit unterschiedlichen räumlichen und visuellen Sequenzen. So behandelt das Filmmuseum thematisch die auch für den Film relevanten Parameter Bewegung und Licht. Sie geben der äußeren Gestalt ihre Identität und steigern die Wahrnehmung und das Erleben des Gebäudes an diesem spezifischen Ort. Räumlicher und funktionaler Mittelpunkt des multifunktionalen Gebäudes ist die zentrale „Arena" in Form eines abgetreppten Foyers. Sie stellt die Schnittstelle zwischen dem Außenraum und den unterschiedlichen internen Nutzungen dar und ist ebenso lichtdurchfluteter Treffpunkt, Bühne, Ruhebereich, Aussichtsplattform, Bar, Café, Restaurant und Wohnraum.

Véritable sculpture en plein air, le musée du cinéma d'Amsterdam occupe une situation dégagée face à la vieille ville et à la gare principale, sur un coude de l'IJ, en un point où se rencontrent la terre et la mer. Visible de loin, il constitue un signal architectural dans ce nouveau quartier qui se crée au nord. Son corps horizontal et dynamique complète la tour Shell voisine. Dans le jeu changeant des rapports de lumière, sa géométrie cristalline, configuration légère, change sans cesse d'aspect. Le chemin depuis le centre-ville correspond à une dramaturgie dont les différentes séquences spatiales et visuelles se mettent en scène dans une approche captivante. Par là, le Filmmuseum traite une thématique indissociable de l'art cinématographique, les paramètres du mouvement et de la lumière. Ceux-ci confèrent à son aspect extérieur une identité et renforcent la perception et le vécu du bâtiment en ce lieu spécifique. L'« arène » centrale, un hall à gradins, constitue le point focal spatial et fonctionnel de ce bâtiment polyvalent. Elle est l'interface entre l'espace extérieur et les différentes utilisations intérieures, mais aussi un point de rencontre inondé de lumière, une scène, un lieu de repos, une plate-forme panoramique, un bar, un café, un restaurant et un espace de vie.

Como una escultura exenta, el museo cinematográfico se encuentra en un lugar muy visible frente al casco antiguo y la estación central en una curva de la IJ, en tránsito directo entre tierra firme y agua. Aquí actúa como signo visible de una nueva área de desarrollo urbano en el norte de Ámsterdam. Su cuerpo dinámico dispuesto en horizontal complementa la vecina torre Shell. En el juego cambiante de las condiciones lumínicas, la geometría cristalina como configuración ligera se manifiesta cada vez de un modo diferente. Todo el itinerario que se recorre viniendo desde el centro urbano responde a una dramaturgia, cuyas diferentes secuencias espaciales y visuales se escenifican como una sugestiva aproximación. El museo cinematográfico maneja así temáticamente los parámetros de movimiento y luz, que tan relevantes son también para la cinematografía. Estos proporcionan su identidad a la forma externa e incrementan la percepción y experiencia del inmueble en ese lugar específico. Como foco espacial y funcional de este edificio polivalente, la "arena" central actúa en forma de vestíbulo escalonado. Constituye un punto de contacto entre el espacio exterior y las instalaciones internas y es al mismo tiempo refulgente punto de encuentro, escenario, zona de descanso, plataforma panorámica, bar, café, restaurante y sala de estar.

Il Museo del film si trova esposto come una scultura in una posizione ben visibile, di fronte al centro storico e alla stazione centrale, laddove la curvatura dell'Ij segna il passaggio dalla terra all'acqua. Qui esso funge da segnale, evidente anche da lontano, di una nuova zona di sviluppo urbano al nord di Amsterdam. Il suo corpo dinamico orientato orizzontalmente costituisce un completamento della vicina torre Shell. Nel gioco cangiante delle condizioni di luce, la sua geometria cristallina di leggera conformazione presenta un aspetto sempre nuovo. Tutto il cammino dal centro della città al museo equivale ad una drammaturgia, le cui sequenze spaziali e visuali mettono in scena un avvicinamento emozionante. Così il Museo del film tratta tematicamente i parametri di movimento e luce, essenziali anche per il film. Questi conferiscono alla figura esteriore una propria identità e aumentano la percezione e l'esperienza del fabbricato sul posto. L'"arena centrale", sotto forma di un foyer con le scale, agisce da fulcro spaziale e funzionale dell'edificio multifunzionale. Essa coniuga lo spazio esteriore e i diversi impieghi interni ed è allo stesso tempo luminoso punto d'incontro, palcoscenico, luogo di riposo, piattaforma panoramica, bar, caffè, ristorante e soggiorno.

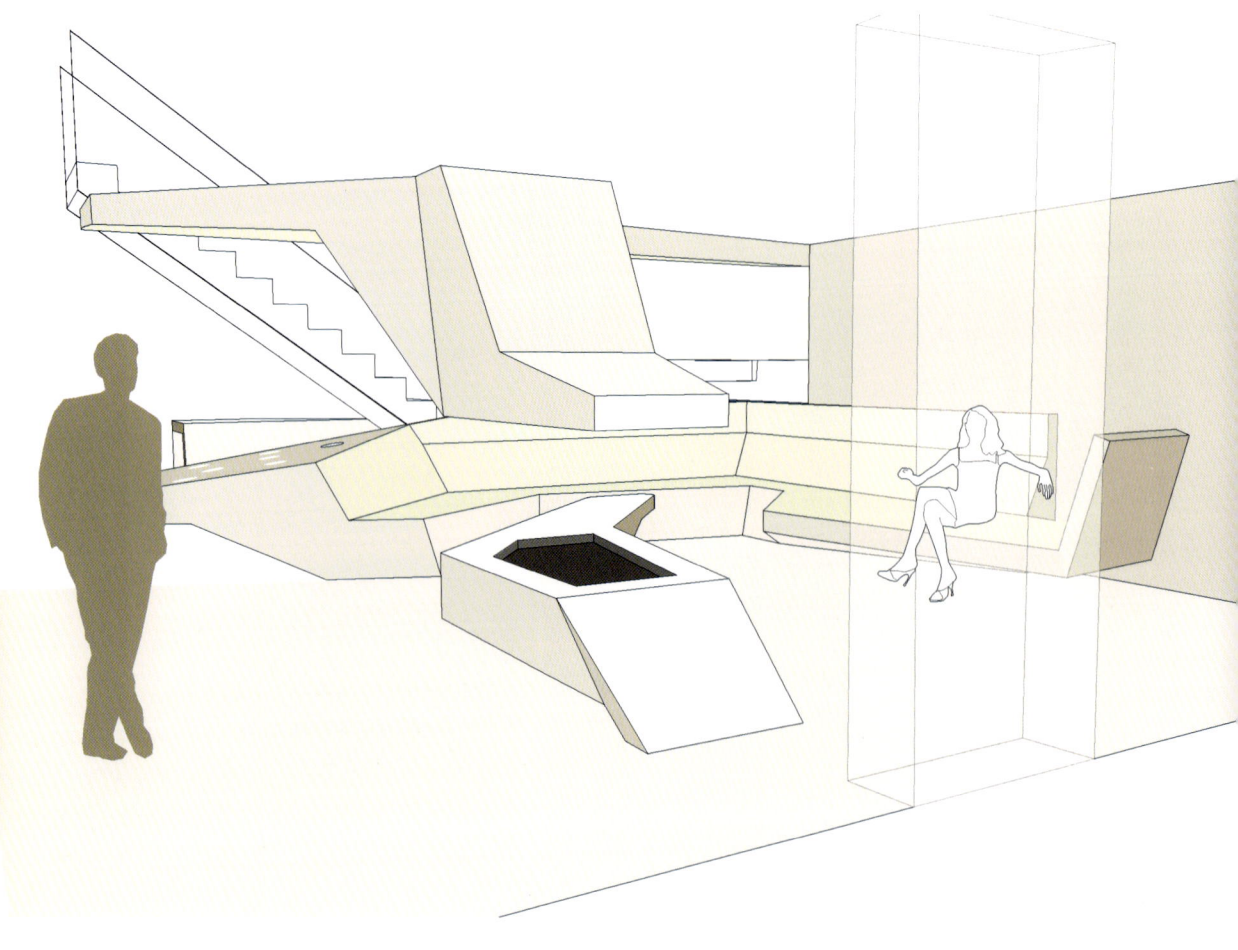

APARTMENT OBERLECH
INTERIOR DESIGN | VORARLBERG
Client: Private
Construction period: 2006-2007
Floor area: 250 m²

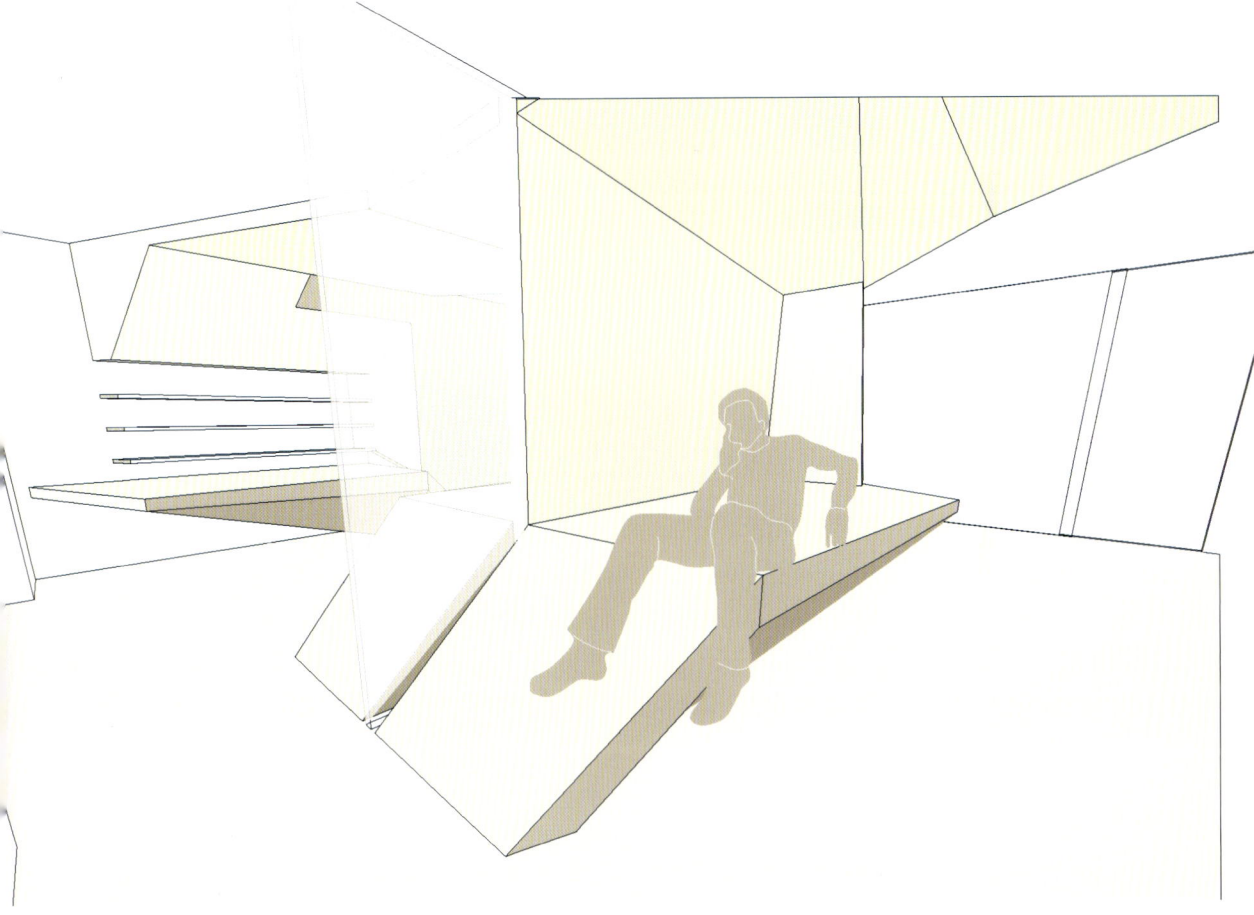

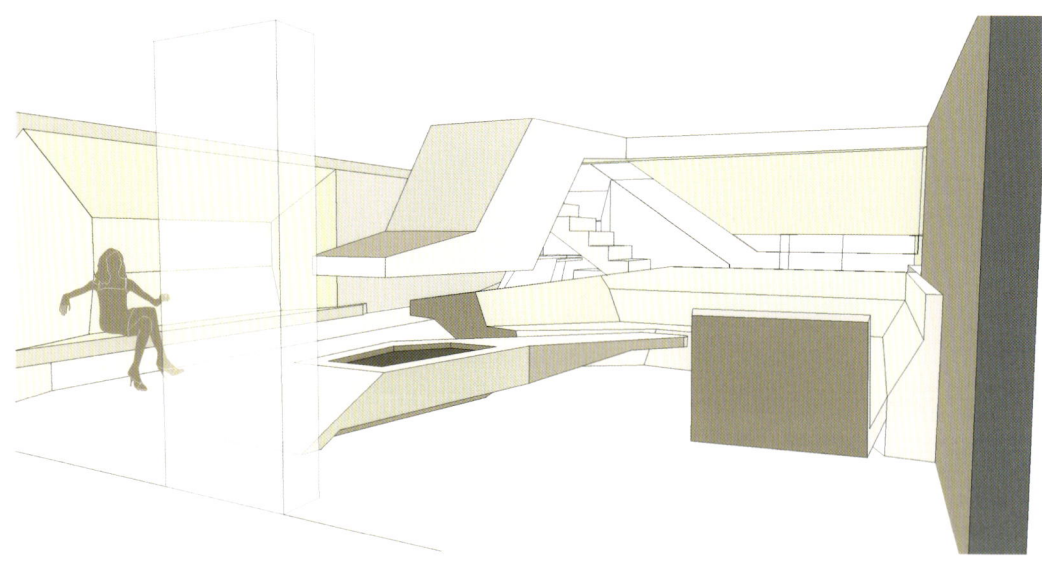

The Viennese office was contracted to develop the interior design of a holiday flat on the basis of an existing plan in the traditional and glamorous skiing resort in the Vorarlberg region. The very narrow ground plot is home to the residential unit which is spread over three stories. The design reflects the users' needs for peace and quiet, privacy and relaxation in order to properly finish off a strenuous day on the slopes in a fitting atmosphere. The interior is kept in warm earthen colours which successfully create a comfortable and snug feeling. They also serve to underline the contrast to the white, cold environment outside. There are no harsh borders between individual rooms but instead they flow into each other seamlessly.

The entrance is on the upper storey, on which level you will also find the bedrooms. The room-sized berths shape all furnishings as if out of a mould. The lower floor houses the living quarters. A generously sized fireplace opens up a sweeping and extensive relaxation area. The materials for the sauna, steam bath and rest areas in the basement were also chosen with the utmost care.

Im traditionsreichen mondänen Vorarlberger Skiort wurde das Wiener Büro mit der Innenraumgestaltung einer Ferienwohnung auf Grundlage einer bestehenden Planung beauftragt. Die Wohneinheit erstreckt sich auf einem sehr schmalen und tiefen Grundriss über drei Geschosse. Der Entwurf reagiert auf die Bedürfnisse des Nutzers nach Ruhe, Zurückgezogenheit und Entspannung, um einen anstrengenden Skitag in passender Atmosphäre vollenden zu können. Das in warmen Erdtönen gehaltene Interieur zielt auf eine komfortable und behagliche Atmosphäre und unterstreicht den Kontrast zur weißen, kühlen Landschaft. Die Räume weisen keine Grenzen auf, sondern gehen fließend ineinander über.

Man betritt das Gebäude über das obere Hanggeschoss. Auf dieser Ebene liegen auch die Schlafbereiche, die als raumgroße Kojen sämtliche Möbel aus einem Formenverlauf herausbilden. Im 1. Untergeschoss befindet sich die Wohnebene. Hier lädt ein großer Kamin, aus dem sich eine weitläufige Liegelandschaft entwickelt, zum Entspannen ein. Die Materialien wurden hier, wie auch bei der Gestaltung des großzügigen Wellnessbereiches mit Sauna, Dampfbad und Ruhezonen im 2. Untergeschoss, sorgfältig ausgewählt.

L'agence de Vienne s'est vu confier, sur la base d'un projet existant, le soin de concevoir le décor intérieur d'un chalet situé dans ce village de sports d'hiver mondain et riche de tradition du Vorarlberg. L'unité d'habitation s'étend sur trois étages, sur un terrain très étroit et profond. Le projet répond au désir de l'utilisateur de trouver le calme, la retraite et la détente pour achever une éprouvante journée de ski dans une atmosphère adéquate. Les tons chauds de l'intérieur créent une ambiance confortable et agréable, en soulignant le contraste avec le paysage blanc et froid. Les pièces ne sont pas délimitées, mais se succèdent avec fluidité.

L'accès se fait par l'étage supérieur. À ce niveau se trouvent également les aires de repos, qui forment l'ensemble du mobilier en tant que cabines de la taille de la pièce. Les pièces à vivre se trouvent au niveau inférieur. Ici, une grande cheminée invite à se détendre sur les sièges qui l'agrémentent. Au rez-de-chaussée consacré à la remise en forme, les matériaux du sauna, du bain à vapeur et des aires de repos ont été choisis avec tout autant de soin.

El despacho de Viena recibió el encargo de llevar a cabo el diseño interior de un proyecto ya existente en Vorarlberg, estación de esquí mundana y de gran tradición. La vivienda se reparte a lo largo de tres pisos levantados sobre una planta muy estrecha y profunda. El proyecto responde a las necesidades del inquilino de encontrar silencio, retiro y relajación para poder concluir una extenuante jornada de esquí en el ambiente apropiado. El interior realizado en cálidos tonos tierra se destina a lograr un ambiente cómodo y acogedor, y pone de relieve el contraste con el paisaje blanco y frío. Las estancias no marcan límites sino que se prolongan las unas a otras con fluidez.

Se entra al edificio por el piso situado en la parte más alta de la pendiente. En ese nivel se encuentran también los dormitorios concebidos como grandes camarotes cuyos muebles surgen en su totalidad a partir de un desarrollo formal. En el primer entresuelo se encuentran las áreas de estar. Aquí, una gran chimenea en torno a la cual se despliega una amplia zona de sofás invita a descansar. Con el mismo esmero se eligieron los materiales del espacioso recinto de wellness situado en el segundo entresuelo con sauna, baño de vapor y zonas de relajación.

Lo studio viennese è stato incaricato di occuparsi dell'interior design di un appartamento per vacanze in questa località sciistica di carattere mondano nel Vorarlberg, partendo da un progetto già esistente. L'unità abitativa consiste di tre piani su una superficie molto stretta e bassa. Il disegno asseconda le esigenze di quiete, isolamento e tranquillità dell'utente, permettendogli di concludere una stancante giornata di attività sportiva nell'atmosfera giusta. L'interno a colori terra caldi è mirato a creare un ambiente comodo e accogliente e sottolinea il contrasto con il paesaggio bianco e freddo. Le stanze non hanno confini, ma si aprono l'una nell'altra in maniera fluida.

Attraverso il piano superiore, il più alto sul pendio, si accede all'edificio. A questo livello si trovano anche le stanze da letto, in cui, come in cuccette di grandi dimensioni, tutti i mobili sono il prodotto di uno sviluppo di forme. Al primo piano inferiore si trova la zona giorno. Qui, davanti a un grande caminetto, si apre un ampio spazio dotato di divani che invita al relax. Altrettanto accuratamente sono stati scelti i materiali per l'ampia zona wellness con sauna, bagno turco e spazi riposo al secondo piano inferiore.

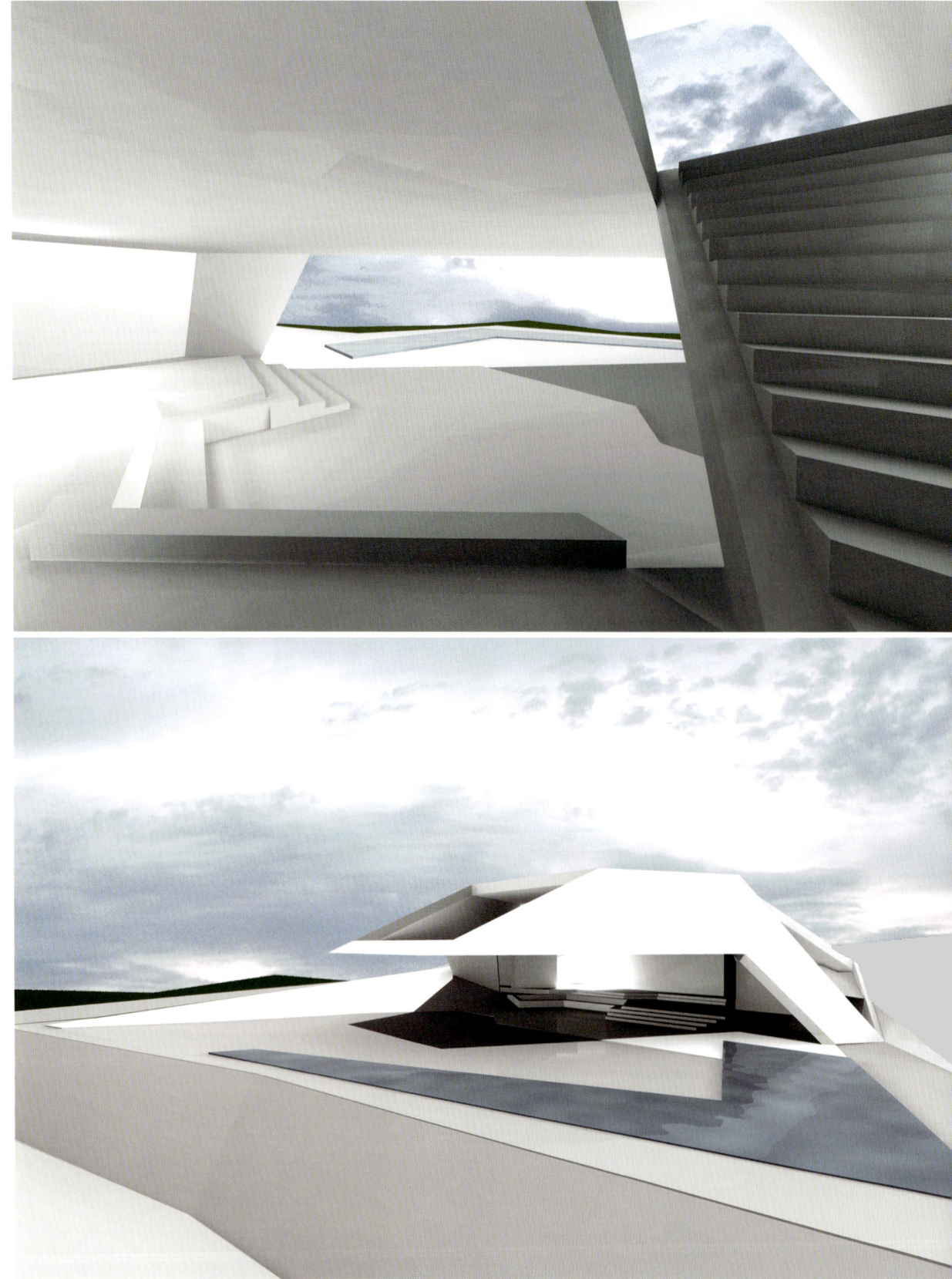

HOUSE OEDBERG

VIENNA 2005
Competition
Awarding body: Private
Floor area: 412 m²
Site area: 1.300 m²

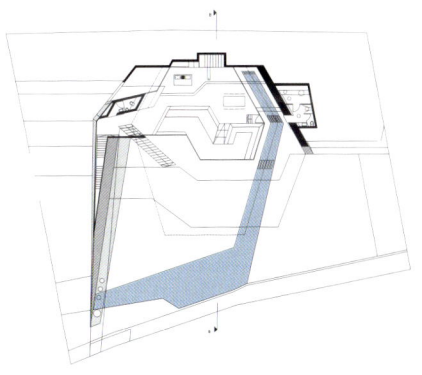

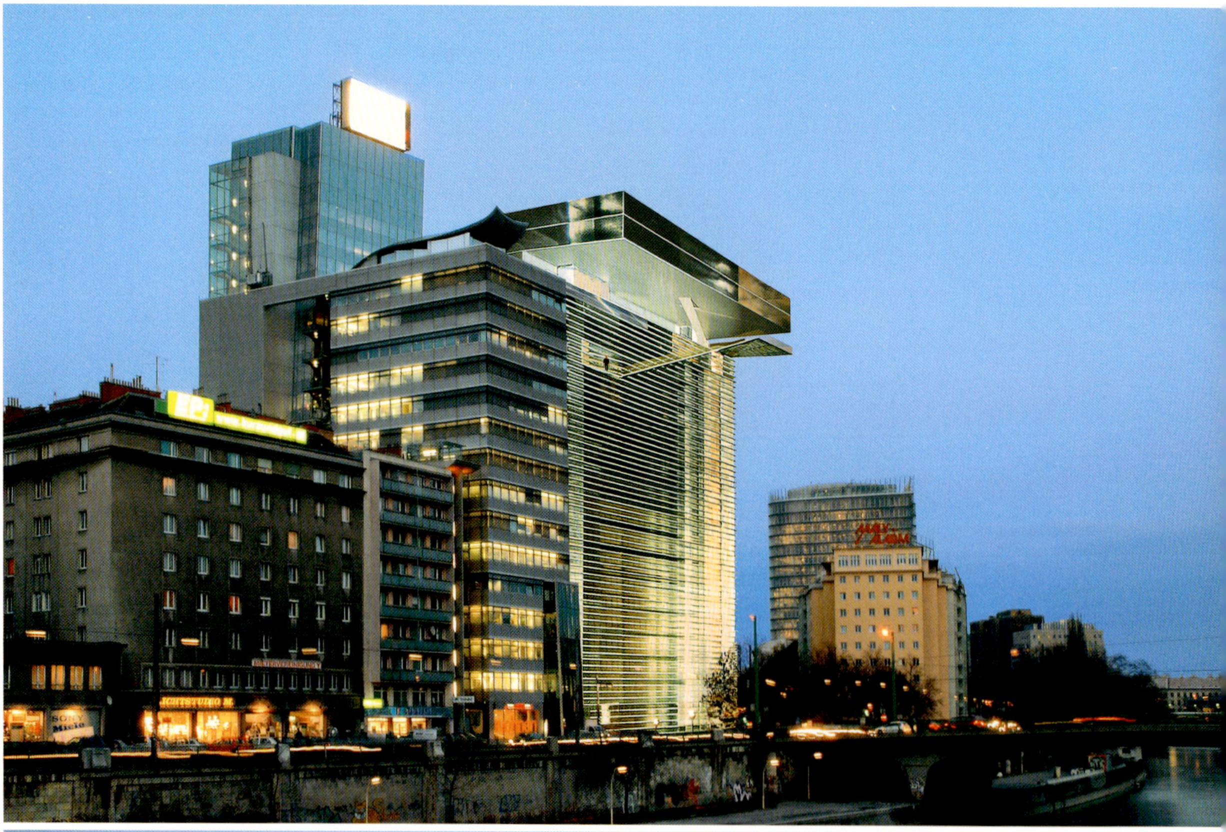

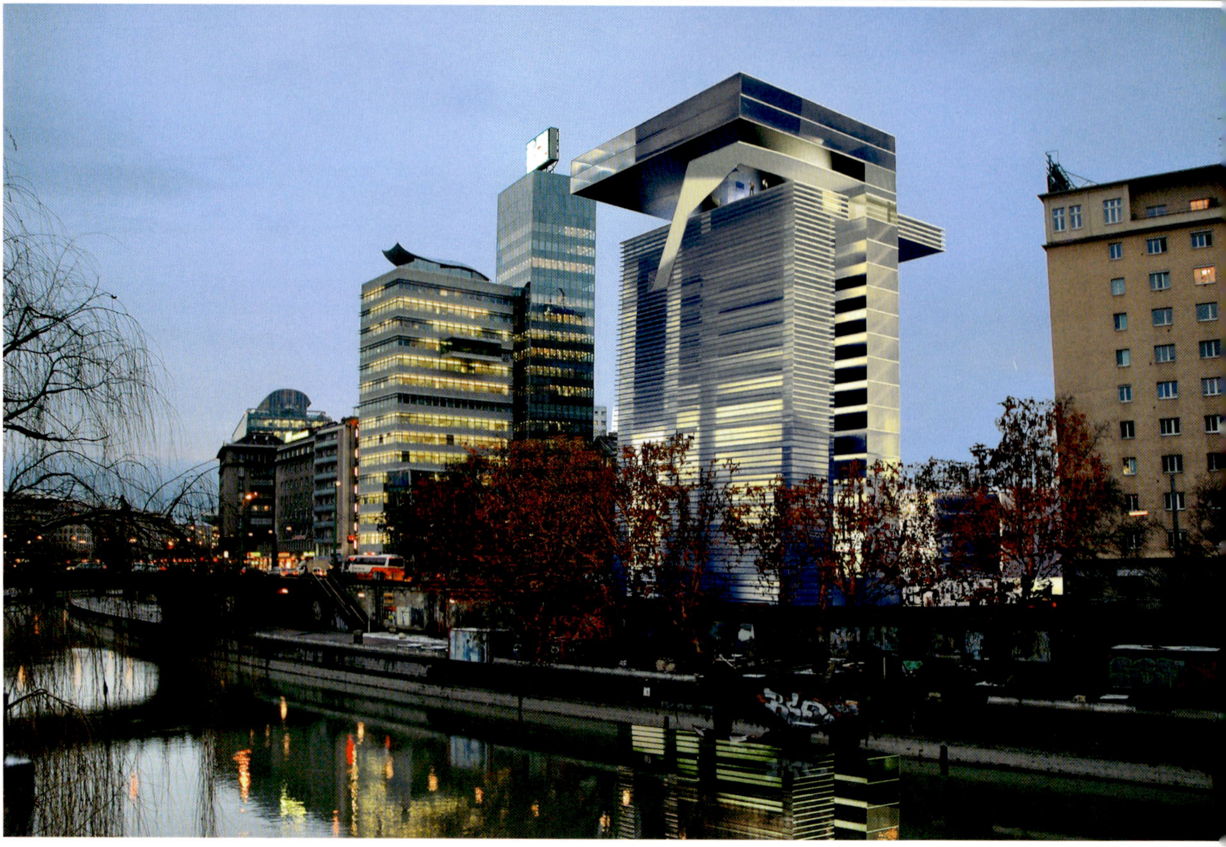

UNIQA TOWER
VIENNA 2005
Competition
Awarding body: UNIQA Versicherungen AG
Floor area: 26.038 m^2

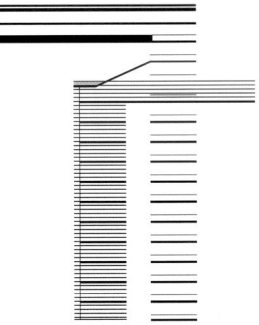

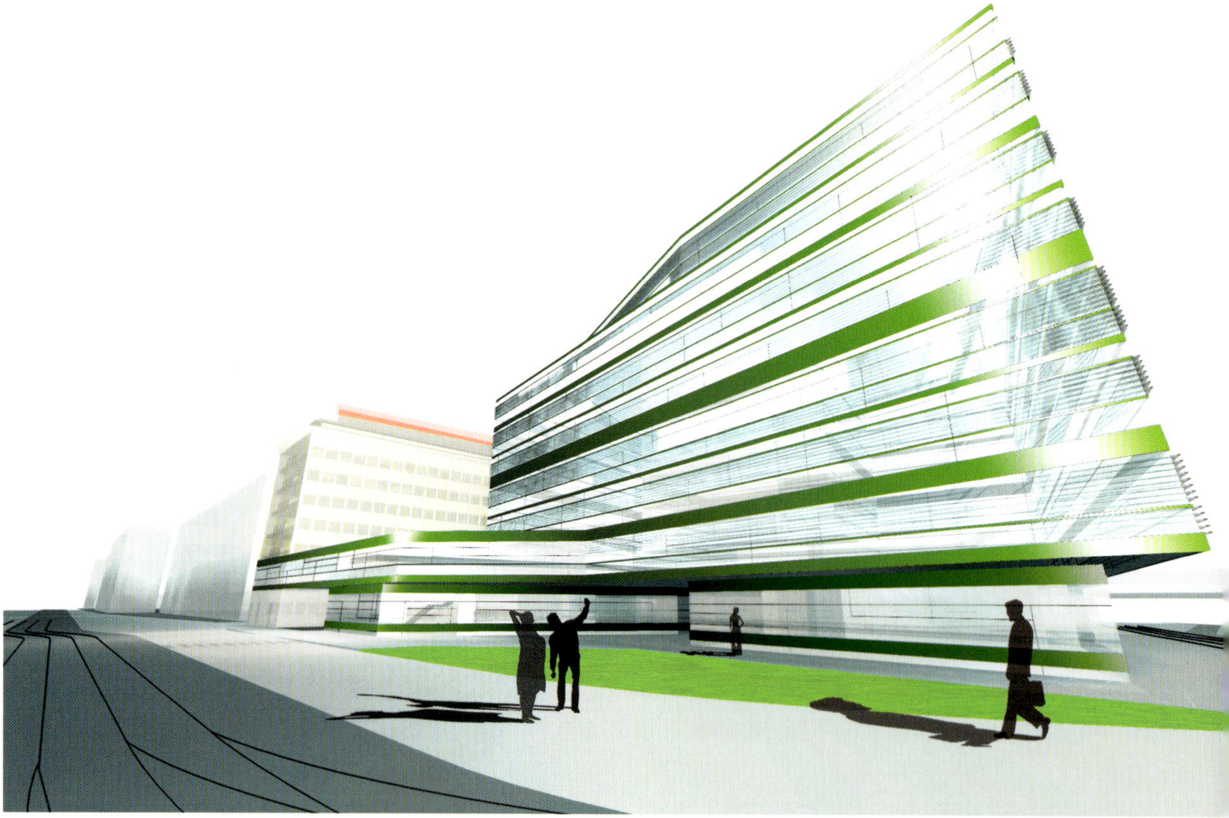

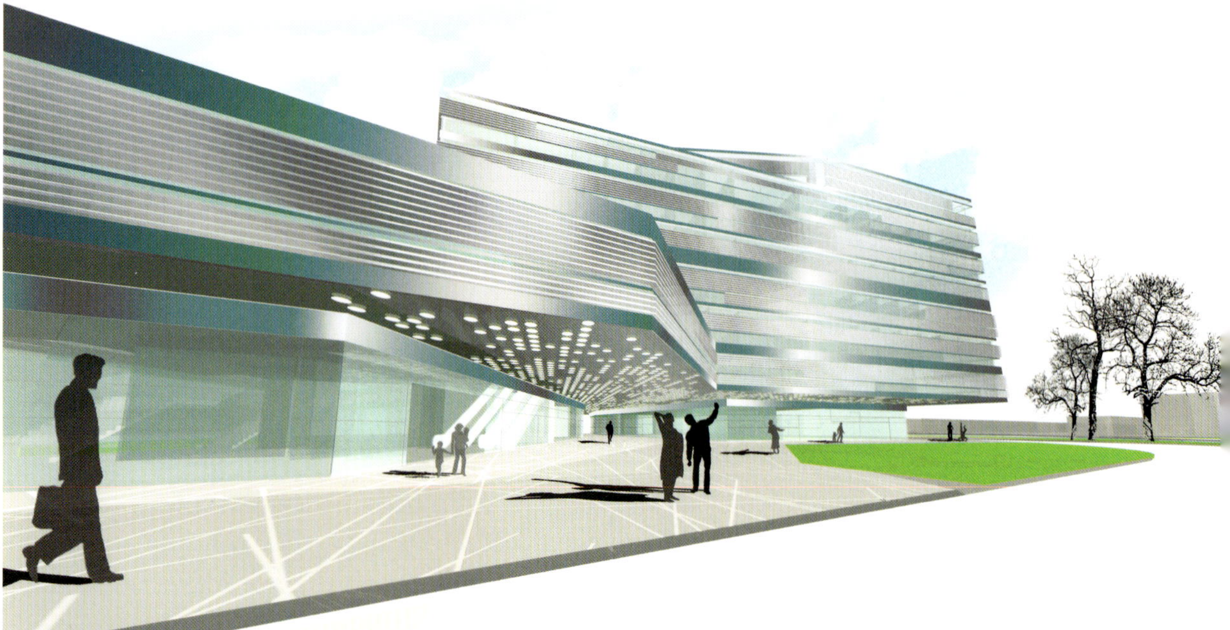

OFFICE BUILDING PRATERSTERN
VIENNA 2004
Competition: 2nd Prize
Awarding body: ÖBB
Floor area: 15.266 m^2

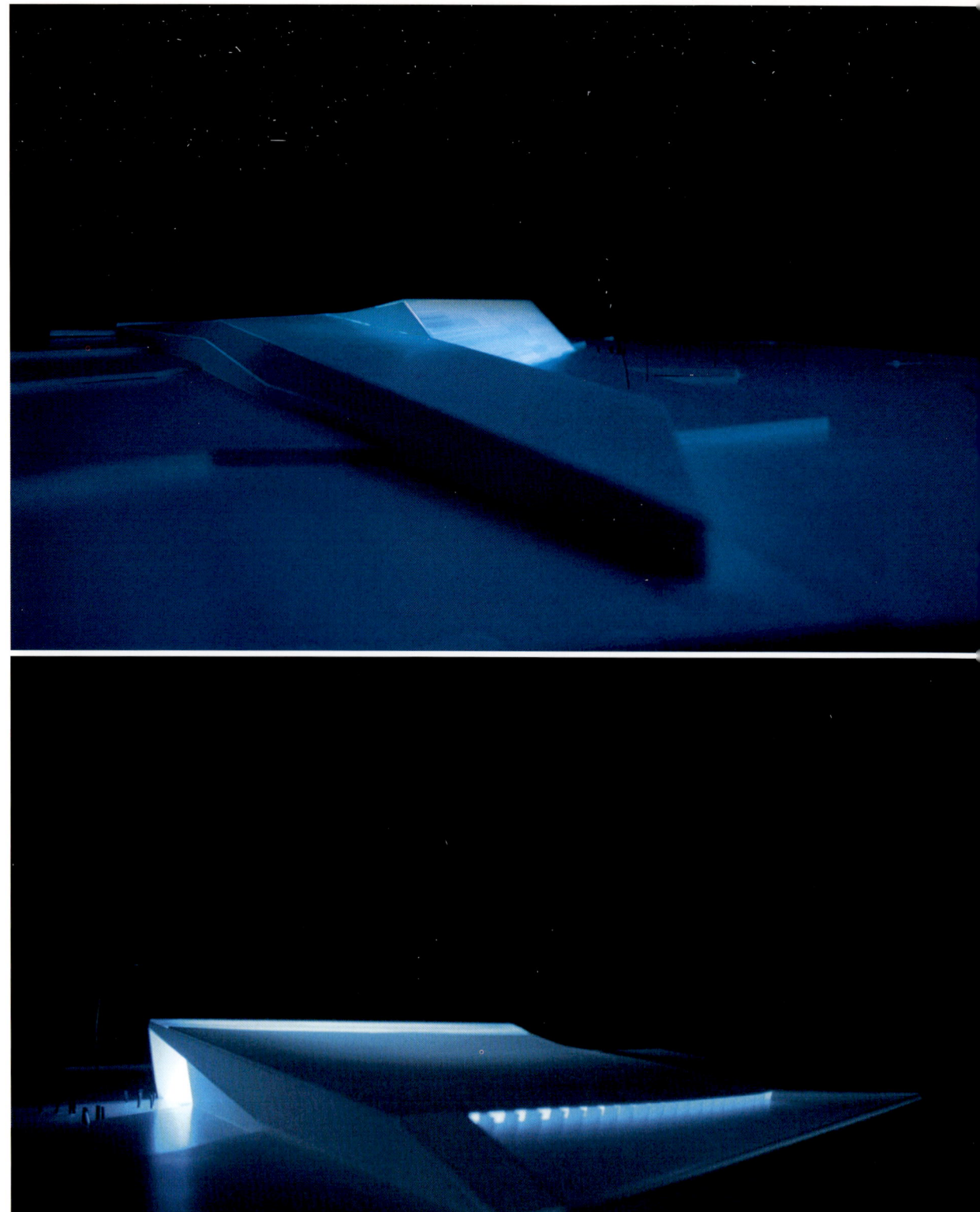

ADI DASSLER BRAND CENTER
HERZOGENAURACH 2004
Competition: 1st Prize group
Awarding body: Adidas Salomon AG
Floor area: 10.387 m^2

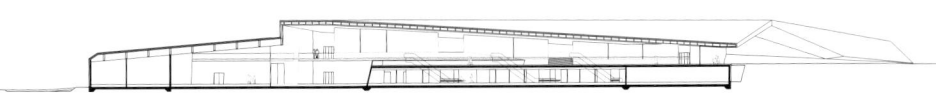

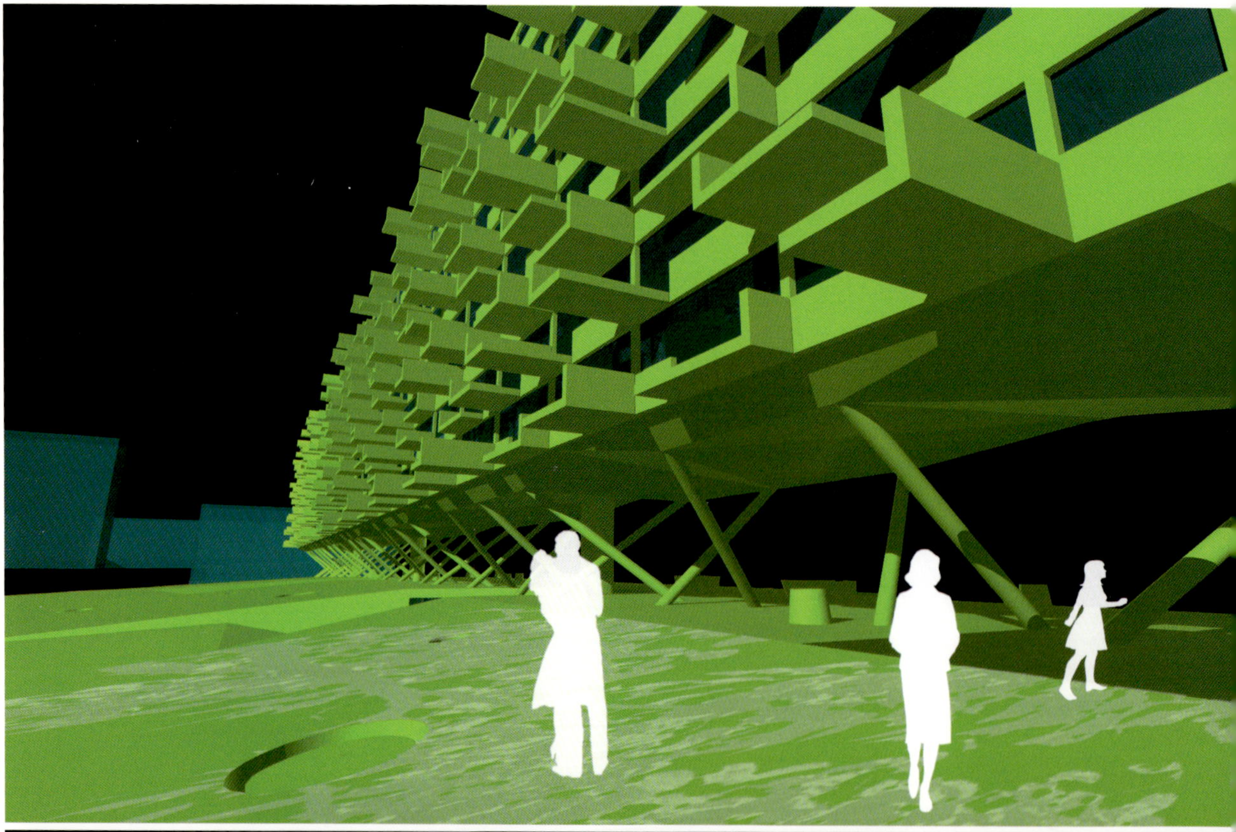
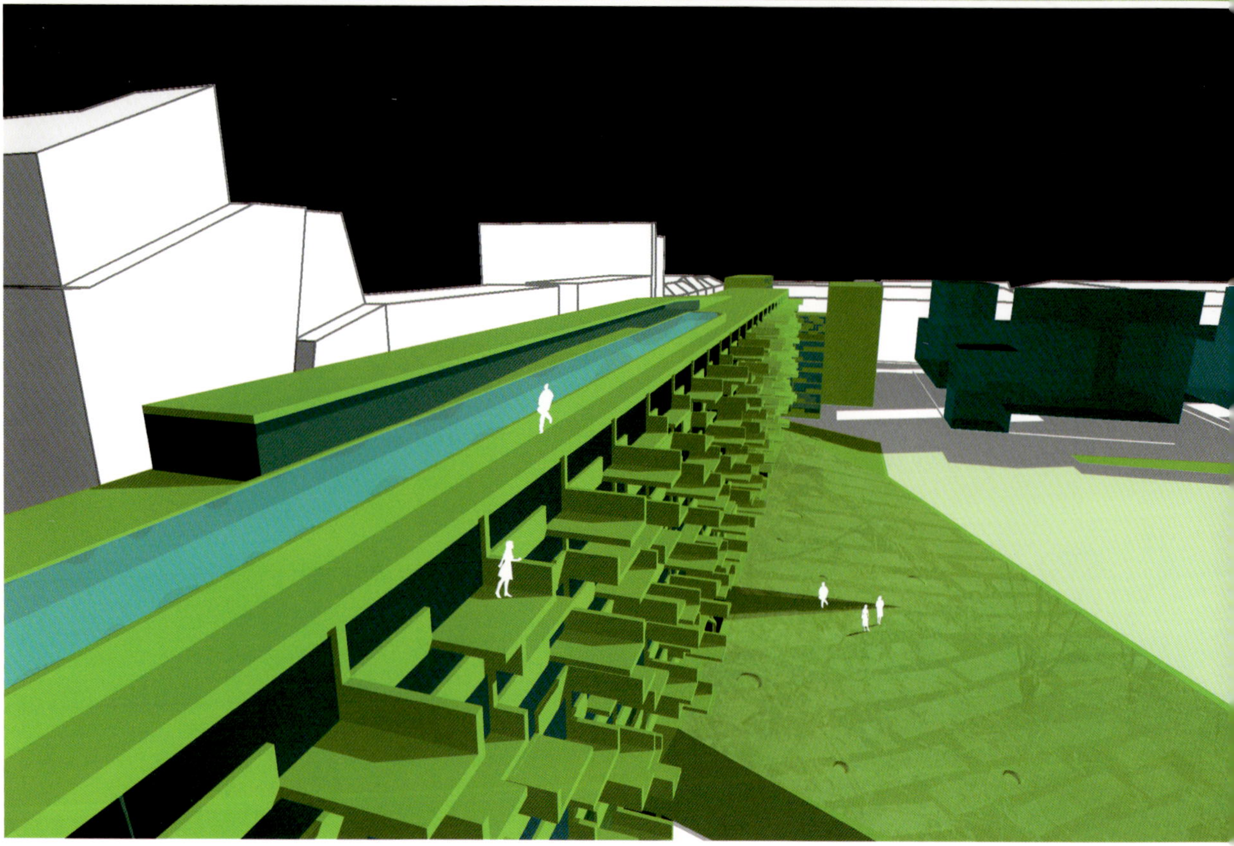

PARKSIDE APARTMENTS
VIENNA 2003
Competition
Awarding body: GESIBA, Wien + Stadt Wien MA 21A
Floor area: 34.011 m^2
Building length: 192 m

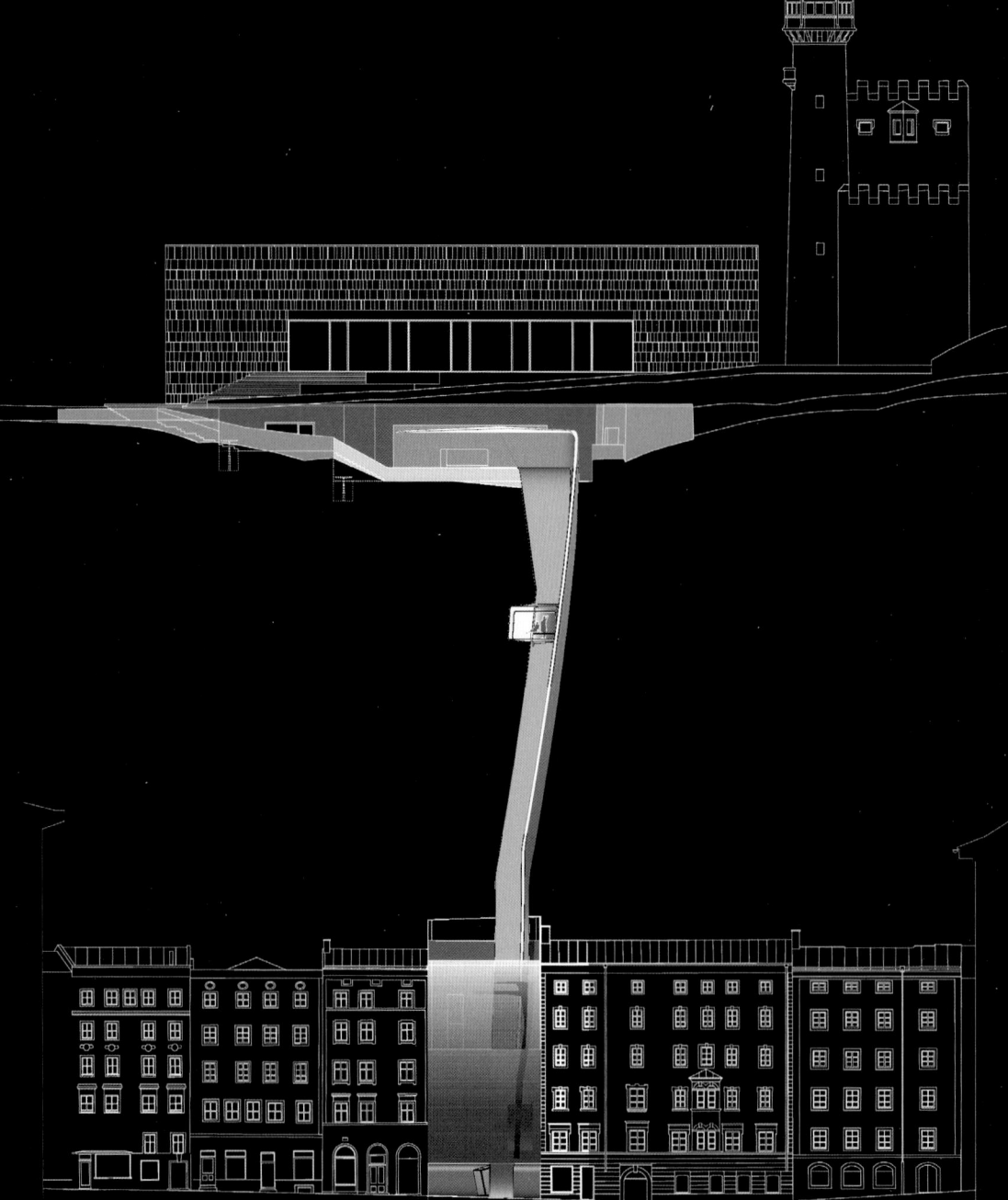

PANORAMA LIFT MÖNCHSBERG
SALZBURG 2003
Competition: 1st Prize
Awarding body: Salzburg AG
Height: 60 m

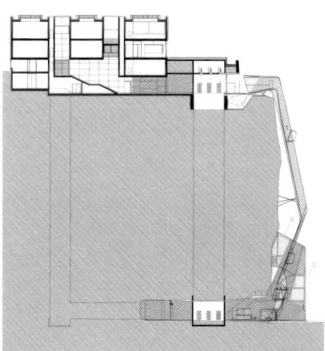

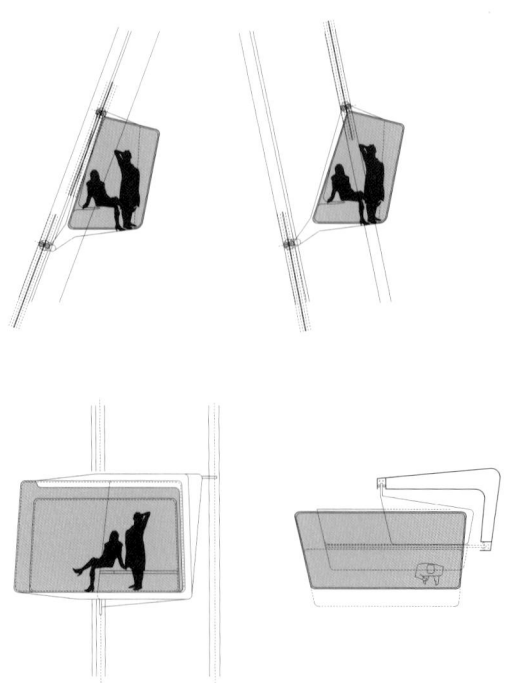

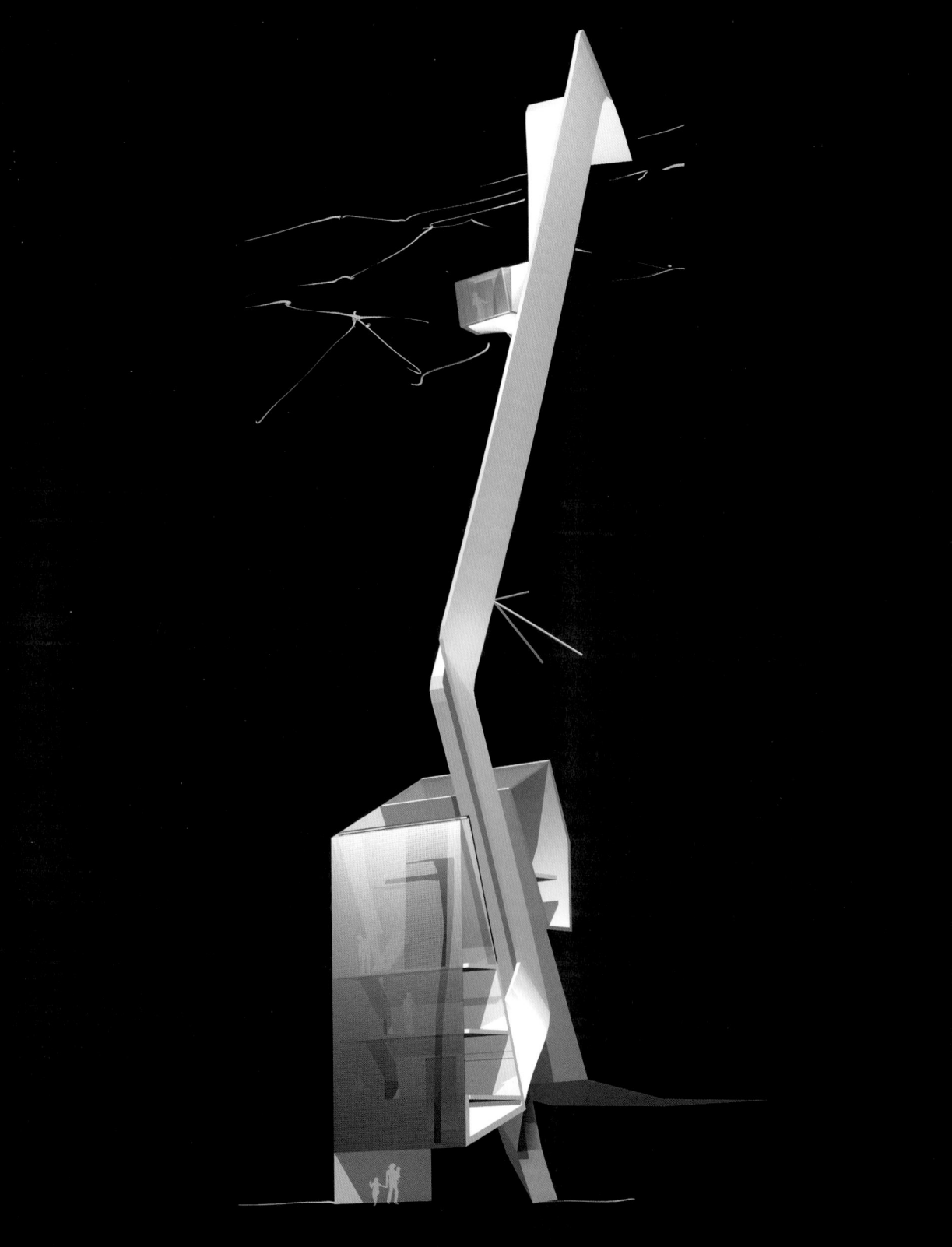

OMV ADMINISTRATION BUILDING
VIENNA 2001
Competition: 2nd Prize
Awarding body: OMV AG
Floor area: 29.937 m^2

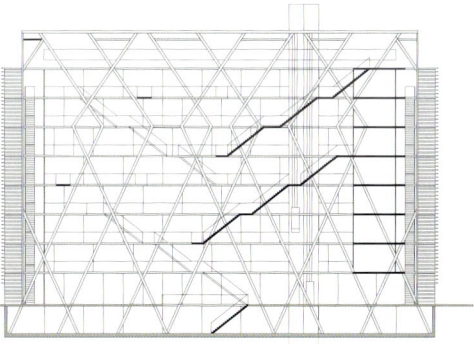

DON GIL FLAGSHIPSTORE
GRAZ 2000
Competition: Awarded
Awarding body: Don Gil Textilhandels AG
Floor area: 563 m^2

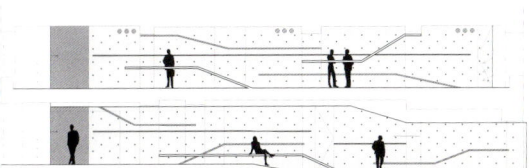

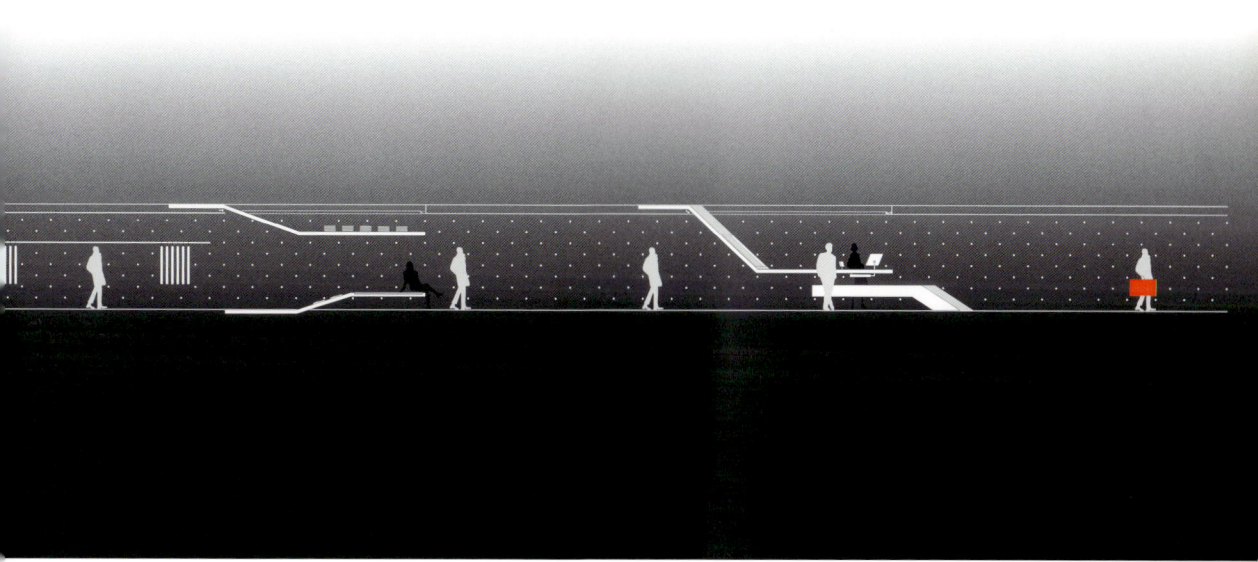

SIGNAL BOXES FOR THE FEDERAL AUSTRIAN RAILWAYS
VIENNA 2000
Competition
Awarding body: ÖBB
Floor area: 1.351 m^2

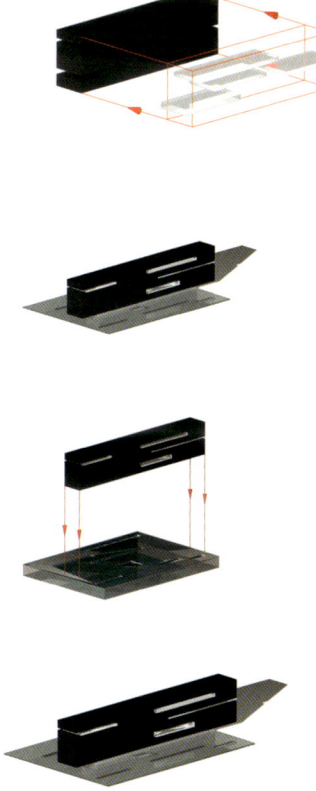

INTERNATIONAL AIRPORT + TOWER
VIENNA 1999
Competition: 2nd Prize
Awarding body: Flughafen Wien AG
Floor area: 151.940 m^2

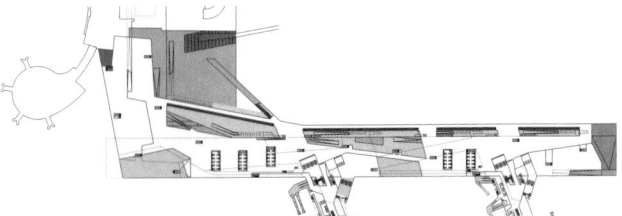

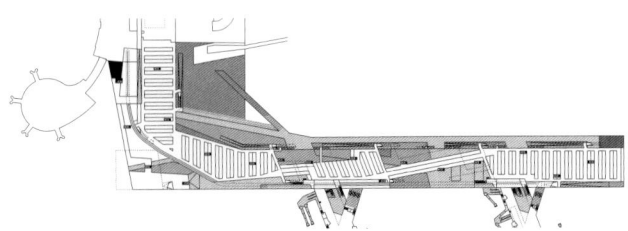

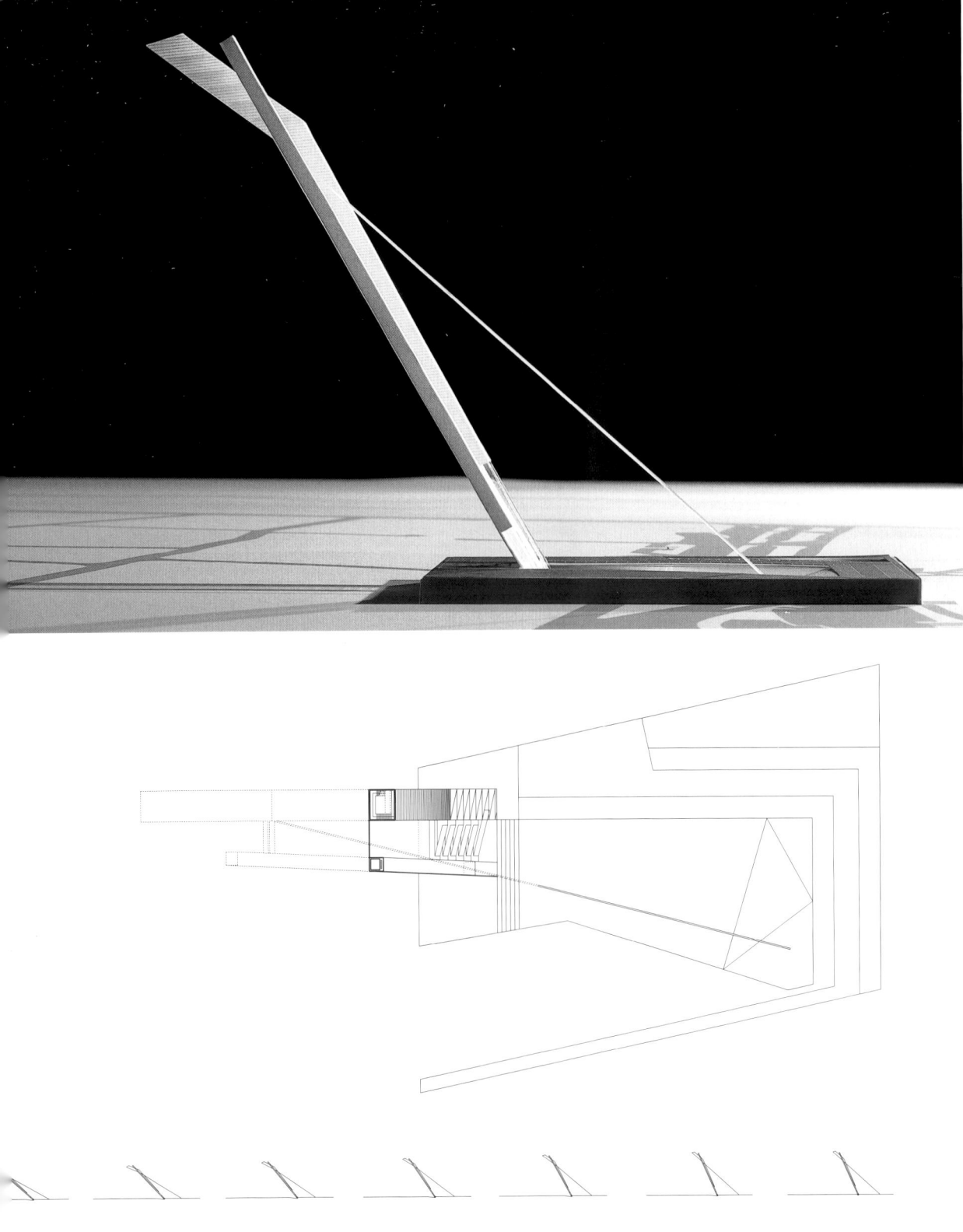

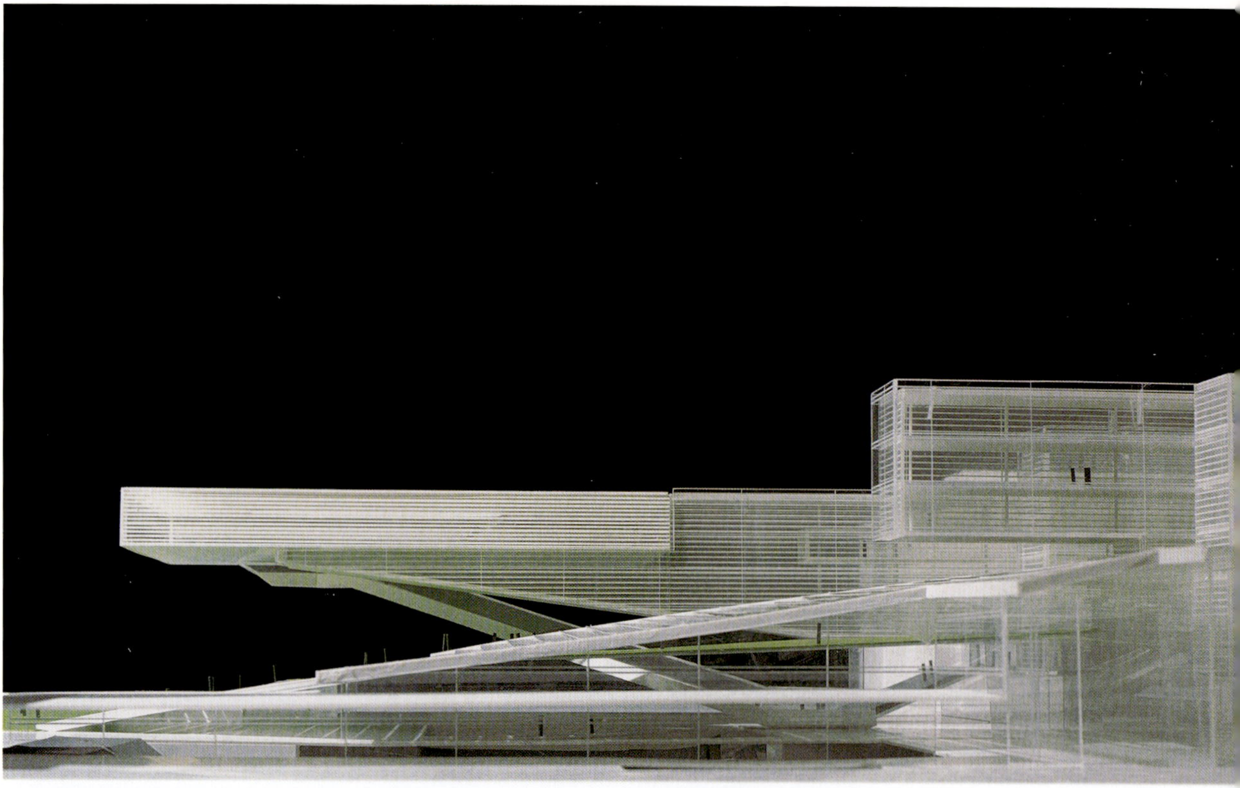

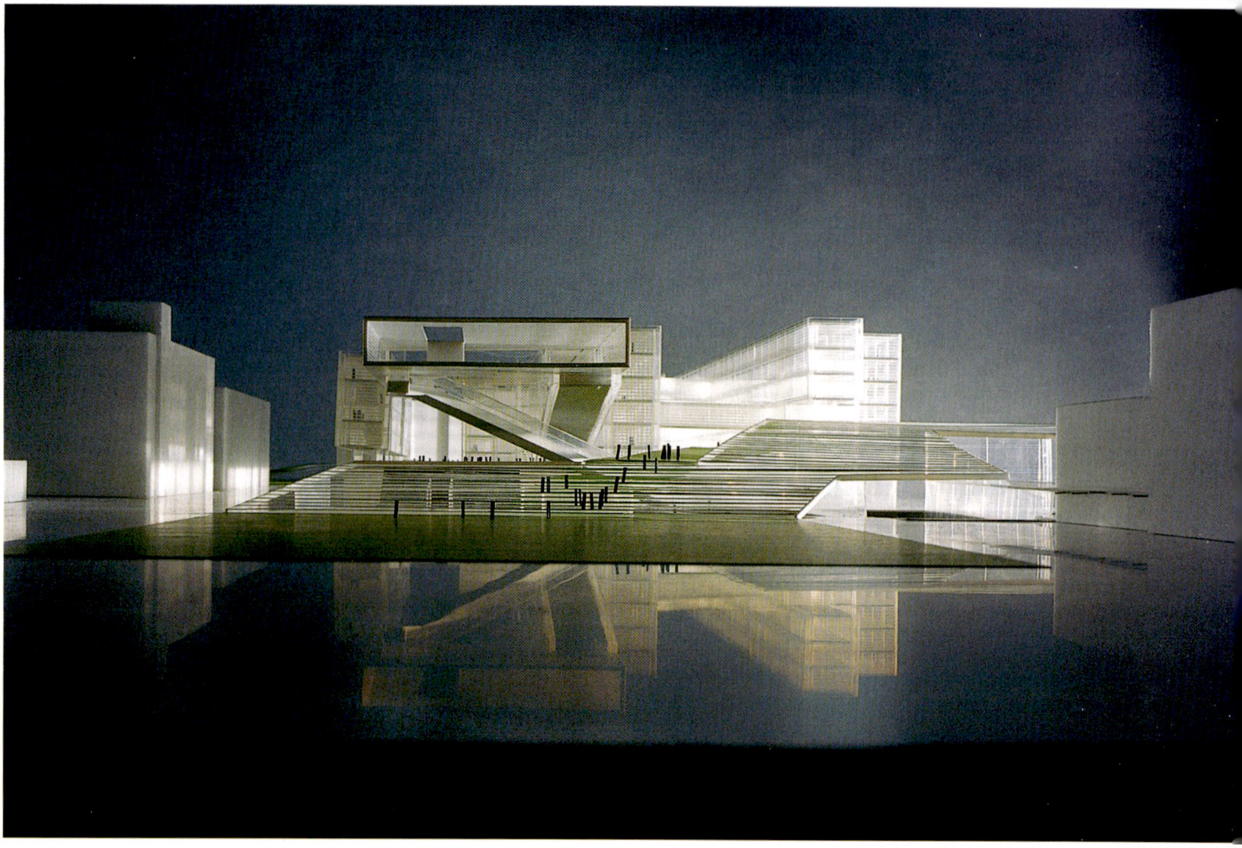

TRAIN STATION
LINZ 1997
Competition: 3rd Prize
Awarding body: Bahnhof Linz Projektentwicklungs GesmbH
Floor area: 80.900 m^2

TWIN TOWER WIENERBERG
VIENNA 1996
Expert report Wienerberg: 1st Prize ex aequo
Awarding body: Stadt Wien
Floor area: 123.896 m^2

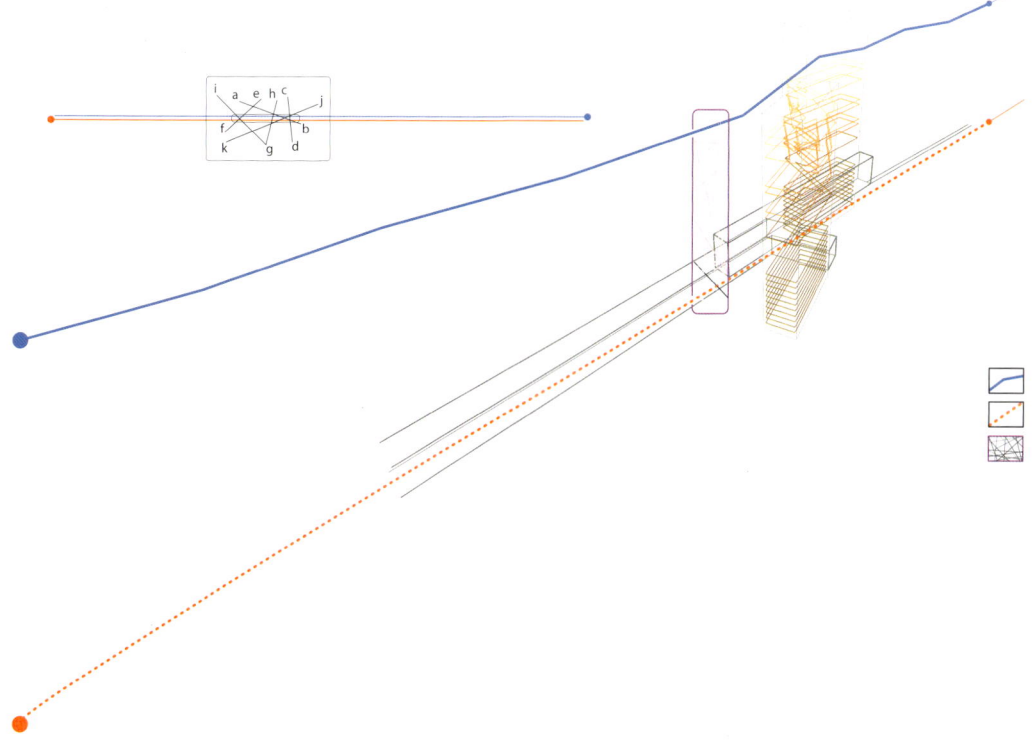

INDEX

DELUGAN MEISSL ASSOCIATED ARCHITECTS
Mittersteig 13/4, A-1040 Wien
P + 43(0)1 5 85 36 90
F + 43(0)1 5 85 36 90 11
office@deluganmeissl.at
www.deluganmeissl.at

Elke Delugan-Meissl

born 1959 in Linz, Austria
Studied at the Polytechnic in Innsbruck and graduated under Professor O. Barth
Various studios in Innsbruck and Vienna, Prof. Wilhelm Holzbauer

Roman Delugan

born 1963 in Merano, Italy
Studied at the Academy of Applied Arts in Vienna and graduated from the
masterclass of Prof. Wilhelm Holzbauer
From 1984 to 1985 he worked on the research project "Architecture of the
20th century in Austria" directed by Friedrich Achleitner
From 1996 to 1997 guest lecturer at the Academy of Applied Arts in Vienna
From 2004 to 2005 guest professor FH Bern, Switzerland

In 1993 they co-founded the architecture studio Delugan_Meissl
In 2004 DELUGAN MEISSL ASSOCIATED ARCHITECTS

Dietmar Feistel

born 1966 in Bregenz, Austria
Studied at the Polytechnic in Vienna
Various Studios in Vienna, Baumschlager & Eberle and Heinz Lindner
From 1996 to 2000 teaching position at the Polytechnic in Vienna, Will Alsop
Since 1998 collaborator and project manager at Delugan Meissl
Since 2004 associate partner at Delugan Meissl Associated Architects

Martin Josst

born 1973 in Hamburg, Germany
Studied at the Muthesius Academy of Art and Design in Kiel, Germany
Collaborator at Morphosis, Los Angeles
Since 2001 collaborator and project manager at Delugan Meissl
Since 2004 associate partner at Delugan Meissl Associated Architects

Christopher Schweiger

born 1971 in Salzburg, Austria
Studies Vienna, Wilhelm Holzbauer, Zvi Hecker and Zaha Hadid
Studies Berlin, Frank Barkow and Peter Baumbach
Since 1996 collaborator and project manager at Delugan Meissl
Since 2004 associate partner at Delugan Meissl Associated Architects

Team

Philip Beckmann, Daniela Hensler, Imke Haasler, Ina Martin, Jörg Rasmussen, Torsten Sauer, Tapio Laßmann,
Burkhard Floors, Ruben Van Colenberghe, Hendrik Steinigeweg, Thomas Hindelang

Realized Projects

Beam, residential development Donaucity, Vienna, Austria 1998

Residential development Oberlaa Vienna, Austria 1998

House J, Absam, Tyrol, Austria 2000

Mischek-Tower, Donaucity, Vienna, Austria 2000

Residential and office building Wimbergergasse, Vienna, Austria 2001

Residential building Paltramplatz, Vienna, Austria 2002

Global Headquarters Sandoz, Novartis Company, Vienna, Austria 2003

House Ray 1, Vienna, Austria 2003

Kallco City Lofts Wienerberg, Vienna, Austria 2004

Apartment Unit 8-II, "Deep Surface", Phoenix City, Beijing, China 2004

Apartment High-rise Wienerberg, Vienna, Austria 2005

House RT, Austria 2005

Current projects

e-Businesspark, Simply 11 Simmering, Vienna, completion: 2008

Residential building Seitenberggasse, Vienna, completion: 2008

Residential building Steigenteschgasse, Vienna, completion: 2006

Residential building Simmering, Vienna, completion: 2008

Roof extension Fleischmarkt, Vienna, completion: 2008

House Mödling, Vienna, completion: 2006

House H-L, Vienna, completion: 2007

Apartment Oberlech, completion: 2007

Casa Invisibilis, Vorarlberg, completion: 2007

Residential building Florianigasse, Vienna, completion: 2007

Porsche Museum Stuttgart, completion: 2007

FH Campus Vienna, completion: 2009

Film Museum Amsterdam, completion: 2009

Chair "Serpente", completion: 2006

Competitions (selection)

1993   Psychiatric hospital Wagner Jauregg, Linz, award

Habitation Donaucity, Vienna, 1st prize ex aequo

1995   Habitation Oberlaa, Vienna, 1st prize

1996   Urban design competition Wienerberg, Vienna, 1st prize ex aequo

Military office complex HVZA, Salzburg, prize of the jury

Habitation Hödlgasse, Vienna, 1st prize

Habitation „In der Wiesen Nord", Vienna, 2nd prize

1997   Habitation Plainstrasse, Salzburg, 3rd prize

Train station, Linz, 3rd prize

1998   Industrial building Austria Tabak, Linz, 2nd prize

Galaxy Office Tower, Vienna, 2nd prize

1999   Airport Vienna, 2nd phase, 2nd price ex aequo

Habitation Wienerberg, Vienna, 1st prize

Residential high-rise Wienerberg, lot C, Vienna, 1st prize

2000   „Haus der Zukunft" / "House of the future", 1st prize

Headquarters Italian Space Agency, ASI, Rome

Mautner Markhof, Vienna, 2nd prize

Don Gil Flagshipstore, Vienna

2001   Ice hockey stadium, Innbruck, Award

OMV administration building, Vienna, 2nd prize

Media City Port, Hamburg, 4th prize

Business Park, Simmering, 1st prize

2002   Global Headquarters Novartis Generics, 1st prize

2003   Panoramic elevator, Salzburg, 1st prize

A1 Image Sphere, Vienna, 2nd prize

Wohnen am Park, Vienna

2004   Residential building Kufstein, 2nd prize

Adi Dassler Brand Center, 1st prize group

Office building Praterstern, Vienna, 2nd prize

2005   Uniqa Tower, Vienna

Porsche Museum, Stuttgart, 1st prize

FH Campus Vienna, 1st prize

House Oedberg, Vienna

Film Museum Amsterdam, 1st prize

Awards

2002   Wimbergergasse, Bauherrenpreis 2002

2003   Global Headquarters Novartis, Contractworld Award, 2nd prize

House Ray 1, Polydecor Corian Design Award, 1st prize

2004   House Ray 1, Deutscher Umbaupreis, 1st prize

2006   High-rise Wienerberg, The International Highrise Award 2006, Commendation

Exhibitions

1998   plot – gezeichnete Architektur aus Öster-reich, Vienna

1999   Young European Architects, Museo Nacional de Bellas Artes Buenos Aires

Zeichenbau, Vienna

Women technicians from 1900 to 2000, Vienna

2000   Wiener Planungswerkstatt Wien Städtebau – Der Stand der Dinge

Panoramas Europèens, Pavillon de Lârsenal, Paris

Varius-Multiplex-Multiformis, Young European Architects, Biennale Venice

Don Gil, Institut Français de Vienne, Vienna

2001   Austrian architecture today, Bratislava

Austrian Exhibition of Contemporary Art, Shanghai Art Museum, Shanghai

Austrian architecture today, Ljubljana

Beyond Media, Florence

2002   Delugan_Meissl STATE OF FLUX, kunst Meran / o arte

best of wohnbau, Architekturzentrum Vienna

Next, Biennale Venice, 8th International Architecture Exhibition

2003   InAusNach Salzburg, Ringturm Vienna

Contemporary Austrian Architecture, University Prague

Expo Making Waves, Shanghai

Housing in Vienna, Austrian Cultural Forum, New York

Urban Life, Architectural League of New York

Beyond Media 03, Florence

Stand der Dinge, Wohnen in Bern, Bern

2004   Ungewohnt Gewohnt, Bielefelder Kunstverein, Bielefeld

Rock over Barock, Kunsthaus Muerz

1st International Architectural Biennial Beijing, Apartment Unit 8-II, Peking

Picturing the Modern World: The Photography of Dwell, House Ray 1 by Hertha Hurnaus, James Nicholson Gallery, San Francisco

2005   The 2nd International Architecture Biennale Rotterdam The WaterCity

Rock over Barock, Jung & schön: 7 + 2, Aedes East, Berlin

2006   Delugan Meissl Associated Architects inTENSE repose, Dornbirn, Glasgow, London, Manchester, Hamburg, Amsterdam, Berlin

Photocredits

Hertha Hurnaus
Köstlergasse 3/9, A-1060 Vienna
P + 43 (0)1 523 50 64
hehu@hurnaus.com
www.hurnaus.com

Margherita Spiluttini
Schönlaterngasse 8, A-1010 Vienna
P + 43 (0)1 512 59 08
office@spiluttini.com
www.spiluttini.com

Peter Rigaud
Kirchengasse 32/19, A-1070 Vienna
P + 43 (0)1 713 19 17
peter.rigaud@rigaud.at
www.peterrigaud.com

Rupert Steiner
Theobaldgasse 10/13, A-1060 Vienna
P + 43 (0)1 581 95 20
office@rupertsteiner.com
www.rupertsteiner.com

© 2008 daab
cologne london new york

published and distributed worldwide by
daab gmbh
friesenstr. 50
d - 50670 köln

p + 49 - 221 - 913 927 0
f + 49 - 221 - 913 927 20

mail@daab-online.com
www.daab-online.com

publisher ralf daab

creative director feyyaz

layout alexandra zöller
a.zoeller@snafu.de

editorial project by caroline klein
caroline_klein@hotmail.com

caroline klein studied interior design in florence and architecture at
the technical university of munich. she has been working for different
renowned architectural offices as well as a free lance writer, producer
and editor for international architectural magazins and publishers.

text by caroline klein, imke haasler
text passages by christian muhr, robert temel

english translation ingo wagener
french translation virginie de bermond-gettle
italian translation fiammetta ciuffi
spanish translation concepción dueso
translations by durante & zoratti, cologne and caroline klein
copy editing caroline klein

printed in italy, 2nd edition
www.zanardi.it

isbn 978-3-937718-87-3

all rights reserved.
no part of this publication may be reproduced in any manner.